ALMOST WILD CAMPING

50 British campsites
on the wilder side

James Warner Smith

Amy Woodland

Cool Camping and Punk Publishing are trading names of Tripadee Ltd.
The publishers assert their right to use 'Cool Camping' and
'Punk Publishing' as trademarks of Tripadee Ltd.

Almost Wild Camping

This edition published in the UK in 2021 by
Punk Publishing
81 Rivington Street, London EC2A 3AY
tripadee.co
coolcamping.com

A catalogue record of this book is available from the British Library.
ISBN 978-1-906889-45-6

10 8 6 4 2 1 3 5 7 9

Printed in Great Britain by Bell and Bain Ltd, Glasgow

Contents

Introduction

Big tech is taking over. Or so some people like to have us think. My watch talks to my phone, my alarm clock talks to my kettle and TikTok no longer has anything to do with time at all. So how can it be that, in our technology-obsessed world, the nation still loves going camping, the most low-fi holiday of them all?

The answer, of course, is that relying on tech only exaggerates the sense of freedom we get from living without it. Part of the reason we cherish being outdoors in the wild is precisely because it offers a chance to switch off. The digital office on your smartphone now follows you home but it rarely follows you camping, and there are still plenty of campsites where electricity, showers and other such luxuries don't feature. And that's where this book comes in.

Forget the morning yoga classes and onsite bistros of the modern-day campsite. In *Almost Wild Camping* we've tried to find places for people who want to de-camp from civilization, not re-camp to a canvas version of what they already have at home. Ditch the car, grab your gear and head off to find your pitch – it might be on the far end of a tiny island only accessible by boat (see p.134), it might be along the banks of a river estuary (see p.116) or it might just be within cycling distance of London, so well tucked away that no one knows it's there (see p.60). The one thing you can be sure of is it won't be in a busy meadow with the same neighbours you had last year and the year before and the year before that. In fact, don't expect many neighbours at all.

But why not just go wild camping? I hear you ask. If you're alone or with one other, travelling light and really want to get off the grid, then it's a very good question (which is why we've outlined wild camping advice on pp.6–16). But, aside from worrying about the legalities and hunting for an inconspicuous spot, for some there's just that element of uneasiness that, at first, you simply can't shift. For others, meanwhile, the reason can be summed up in two three-letter words – the loo.

I'm not here to cast aspersions. Having wild camped in Alaska, listening out for bears, and having camped with family friends in Hertfordshire, listening to a labrador snoring in my tent, I know that different occasions call for different campsites and there is, thankfully, plenty of variety on offer. But when you want to forget the tech, have a campfire and pitch in a wildflower meadow or an ancient woodland, I hope this compendium will be the perfect inspiration. Switch off your phone and take a good leaf through the pages. Digital version not available.

James Warner Smith, Editor

Wild camping

What is wild camping?

Camping outside the bounds of designated campsites is known as wild camping. For some people it's simply camping as it's meant to be; sleeping out under the stars, surrounded by the natural world and, crucially, not by any other noisy people. It's pitching up in a secluded spot that takes your fancy and enjoying a night under canvas in the wild. It's the camping of cowboy films, mountaineers and adventure stories. But how does this translate to the regulated western world?

Is wild camping allowed?

There's a widely held belief that wild camping is not legal in England and Wales but, in fact, there's nothing specifically prohibiting it. The confusion around the laws restricting wild camping is really related to trespass. If the person who owns the land has given you the nod to be there, then there's no problem whatsoever with wild camping, from a legal point of view. It's trespassing on someone else's land that's the real point of contention and, of course, there's not always an easy way to find the owner to ask for permission.

Despite this, there are still a few places where it's generally accepted that wild camping goes on and it's tolerated as long as it is done responsibly (see p.10 for wild camping etiquette). These places tend to be the wilder parts of England and Wales; mountains and high fells where well-equipped hikers might want to spend a night out in order to continue a multi-day adventure. In Scotland, this type of camping on open-access land is more than tolerated; it's a right, enshrined in law (see p.13). The rules may be different depending on where you are, but the responsibilities remain the same and can be neatly summed up in the ethos of 'leaving no trace' which, if followed carefully, can open up more wild camping locations. After all, whisper it quietly, but if you truly leave no trace behind and your stay is suitably undetected, who's to say you were ever actually there?

Where to wild camp

Part of the beauty of wild camping is the solitude; camping out in nature without neighbours or noise, somewhere seemingly untouched by other people; lots of us want that. But unfortunately it's this wide appeal that can become part of the problem. In the quick-click age of the internet, an influential photograph can inspire a lot of people in a short space of time and, even if we all pitch responsibly, if we use the same places over and over again, we can damage what we first came to enjoy. It's not really anyone's fault, it's just an unavoidable fact, but its impact can be quite destructive.

In 2020, the COVID-19 pandemic meant, first, that campsites were closed for long periods and, later, that campsites reduced the number of people they could accept. Demand for pitches soon outstripped supply and many more people than usual took to wild camping. And not always responsibly. There were pleas from bodies that usually tolerate wild camping, including national park authorities and the National Trust, for people to stay away, and the reputation of both wild campers and wild camping took a bit of a beating.

With that in mind, you won't find a string of specific wild camping locations recommended among these pages. And we generally advise giving the top blogs and articles online a bit of a swerve if you're looking for truly untouched locations. Forget following that chiselled YouTuber and embrace your freedom. Remember that part of the joy of wild camping is the solitude, so be brave and strike out on your own rather than congregating with loads of other wild campers. You might be surprised at some of the places you find and even more pleased that you can enjoy them to yourself.

For wider areas where wild camping is allowed see pp.13–16, but generally we suggest grabbing and OS map and seeking out your own wild camping spaces, avoiding those you've seen photographed and shouted about on social media. Most importantly of all, if you find somewhere remarkable, remember to leave no trace, both on the environment and on the internet. Take a look at our wild camping etiquette guide (see p.10) and Going Wild for the Planet (see p.186) to help keep your footprint as ultra-light as the latest wild camping gear.

Should I go wild camping?

Before you grab the tent and slip on your well-worn hiking shoes, it's worth considering the kind of camping experience you're after. What expectations do you have? If the thought of hunting out your own wild camping spot is a little daunting, it might be that the 'almost wild' campsites in this book are a better place to start. There are plenty of campsites with simple facilities, far-flung pitches and ample space that emulate some of the experience of wild camping without the worry of wondering whether you're in the wrong place. A campsite like this might already be wild enough or might just be the stepping stone you need to test the water.

You should also be heading to a designated campsite if your idea of wild camping involves a campfire or a big group of friends. Some of the more sociable things that make camping appealing are simply not compatible with protecting wild spaces and camping incognito. If you want to camp with more than one or two mates, if you need a lot of kit, if you want to drive to your pitch or you want a roaring campfire and late nights singing 'Kumbaya', try the almost wild campsites in this book.

If, on the other hand, you're on foot or bike and are adventuring alone or with just one or two others, wild camping will suit you well. If your adventure takes you off the beaten track with no campsites nearby, if you can fit your kit into a backpack or pannier bag, then there's no reason not to camp wild. The freedom is exhilarating, the views are yours to choose and it's hard to be further immersed in nature. Read up to make sure you understand your rights and responsibilities, pack carefully, pitch well, be sensible and enjoy your nights in the wild. And, if you still want to sing 'Kumbaya' quietly, go ahead, we won't judge you. You'll only have the birds to contend with.

WILD CAMPING KIT LIST

▲ A natural-coloured tent
▲ A good sleeping bag that's suited to the season
▲ A ground mat to insulate you from the cold floor
▲ A camping stove, fuel and a means of ignition
▲ Water or knowledge of water sources and a filtration system
▲ More than enough food for your trip
▲ A head torch and spare batteries
▲ A waterproof and warm clothing
▲ A trowel and plastic bags for waste
▲ Hand sanitiser

Wild camping etiquette

In the world of wild camping, where meals are sometimes slurped from saucepans, the toilet is behind a tree and the nearest thing to a shower is a thunderstorm, the idea of etiquette may seem slightly at odds. But, in fact, when you're camping in the great outdoors, with no nosey campsite warden to tell you what's what, wild camping etiquette keeps the whole thing going.

There are some general dos and don'ts that help wild campers to leave no trace. Some may seem obvious, such as not leaving litter behind, while others are a little less talked about, like what's acceptable when going to the loo. All are worth considering, especially if you're embarking on your very first wild camping trip.

To start with, wild camping should only be done in small numbers and usually for just a single night in any location. That spot should be accessed on foot, on unenclosed land, away from livestock and not in view of homes, gardens or roads – and to avoid sticking out in the landscape, it's best to have a natural-coloured tent that's suitable for the conditions. Take time, too, to find a spot well away from the footpath. No matter how remote you feel, never underestimate how early in the morning dog walkers like to get up and out and put us all to shame. It might have taken you a day of walking and four hours pouring over a map to find the place but somehow, if you're near a footpath, it's Sod's law that someone with their dog will be idling past at 4am.

Pitch late, take down your camp early in the morning and be sure to completely clear the area of any rubbish and belongings when you leave. Even if you find litter that wasn't left by you, stick it in a pocket and take it with you, helping the environment and the reputation of fellow wild campers as you go.

DOS AND DON'TS OF WILD CAMPING

- ▲ **Do** ask for landowner permission where possible
- ▲ **Do not** camp in enclosed land near livestock or crops
- ▲ **Do** camp in a natural-coloured tent, away from walkways and roads
- ▲ **Do not** draw attention to your pitch
- ▲ **Do** carry a camping stove to make hot drinks and food
- ▲ **Do not** make a campfire
- ▲ **Do** carry a trowel to dig a toilet
- ▲ **Do not** go to the toilet within 30 metres of water
- ▲ **Do** pick up litter and clear your pitch
- ▲ **Do not** leave any trace of your stay
- ▲ **Do** leave if asked to
- ▲ **Do not** post details of your camping pitch online

For further information, the **Scottish Outdoor Access Code** offers sensible advice for wild campers at **outdooraccess-scotland.scot**.

"You need to be aware that whilst you might visit a place only occasionally and feel that you cause no harm, the land manager or the environment might have to cope with the cumulative effects of many people. Acting with awareness and common sense underpins responsible behaviour."

The Scottish Outdoor Access Code

Water and waste

If you're unable to carry all the water you need for your trip, you might want to choose a wild camping spot close to a water source so you can stock up overnight – but don't get too close. Make sure you pitch above the high water mark, if you're camping on a beach or near tidal water, and be aware of the weather conditions that may cause water levels in streams, rivers or lakes to rise.

If you're using a natural source for your drinking water, it goes without saying that you won't want to pollute it. Washing up liquid or any toiletries you might be taking should be biodegradable, and any solutions containing them should be well diluted and emptied on to the ground rather than directly into the water to maximise the time it has to biodegrade. The main thing to be careful about near a water source, however, is going to the loo.

Let's face it, if you're camping out for a few days, at some point you are going to need to do more than just 'a watery one' and, when the time comes, the big question is, what should you do about it? There's reams of information online extolling the joys of wild camping but often very little about the practicalities of where to drop your trousers and, er, what exactly to do.

First dig a shallow pit for a toilet as far as possible (and at least 30 metres) from camp and any water source. After that, it's time to enjoy the last great freedom of the wild camping experience – the peppermint-like feel of a cold breeze on your bare backside and a free yoga class courtesy of the great outdoors (that position, my friends, is called 'Mālāsana' or the yogi squat). Finish by covering over any solid deposits (they don't tell you that in yoga class) and take everything else away with you. A trowel for digging, a plastic bag for waste and hand sanitiser should be an essential part of a wild camper's kit. And, as a matter of good manners, never ask someone heading for the woods with a shovel what they're up to.

Cooking and campfires

While there's certainly something primally wild about having a campfire, the damage they do in a natural environment is indisputable. Scorch marks don't fit neatly with the ethos of leaving no trace and fires are best kept for occasions when you're on a campsite and there are designated fire pits, water supplies and safety equipment. When you're wild camping, a fire can pose a threat to the wider surroundings, especially in hot weather. We may not see the big bush fires and forest fires of Australia and North America here in the UK but, partcularly in recent years, there has been a growing number of fires on moors and in open access areas, with some of them attributed to campfires and disposable barbecues. It is far better, when following the wild camping code, to use a camping stove for cooking and to make sure you have warm clothes and sleeping bags than to rely on an open fire.

Wild camping wonderlands

In most parts of the UK, wild camping doesn't always feel like an easy option. Tracking down a landowner, like some sort of nomadic Sherlock Holmes on a camping holiday, is not always easy, and attempting to camp undetected presents a moral and legal dilemma that may not make for a good night's sleep. Thankfully, though, the UK also has some wild camping wonderlands where you can pitch a tent without fear of being moved on starting, of course, with (almost) the whole of Scotland.

SCOTLAND

It's rather convenient for the wild camping clan that the UK's greatest outdoors is in Scotland, where camping wild is a legal right. Scotland has the highest mountains, the biggest forests, the largest expanses of water and the lowest population density in the UK. In short, it's the perfect place to go wild camping. The Land Reform Act 2003 protects access rights across the nation, including camping, and lays out common-sense guidelines for campers to follow in the Scottish Outdoor Access Code.

Scotland's two national parks are a good place to start, though, given their national park status, they're also home to some of the most well-known and pressurised

POPULAR AREAS TO **WILD CAMP** IN SCOTLAND

Consider these notes as warnings as well as recommendations. On a summer weekend, the most well-known wild camping spots tend to be busy, so swerve past the popular pitches in favour of a quieter spot in the same area.

▲ Loch Lomond and the Trossachs National Park

If you want one of the popular lochside spots in the Loch Lomond and the Trossachs National Park between March and September, you'll have to sacrifice a bit of your wild side and head for a campsite or apply for a permit. Our advice is to steer clear and head for somewhere more secluded. Ninety-six per cent of the park's 720 miles is unrestricted, so there are plenty of places to choose from.

lochlomond-trossachs.org

▲ The Cairngorms National Park

Forests, lochs, mountains... this vast national park offers plenty of options. The park's website and signage have thorough advice on how to wild camp safely and with respect for the local wildlife populations (red deer, capercaillie and grouse, to name but a few).

cairngorms.co.uk

▲ Isle of Mull

The Isle of Mull, off the west coast of Scotland, is a 45-minute ferry ride from the mainland. There's a designated wild camping zone on the beach at Calgary Bay, which helps to protect the area's special grassland, and another within the Lochbuie Estate, where the island comes most under pressure from wild campers in summer.

isle-of-mull.net

▲ Isle of Skye

Skye, the largest island of the Inner Hebrides, is connected to the mainland by a bridge and is popular with organised campers and wild campers alike. Experienced walkers often take on the unmarked 79-mile Skye Trail, which crosses the island north to south, and camp along the way.

▲ Shetland

The ferry from the mainland to Shetland, the most northerly outpost of the UK, takes 12 hours but what you'll find there is fewer people and more natural beauty. Wild campers are welcomed – subject to the usual pleas for responsible wild camping and a request for permission to be sought from landowners.

locations. Loch Lomond and the Trossachs is, generally, the most easily accessed, just 45 minutes' drive from Glasgow. It's where the Highlands meet the Lowlands and has 22 lochs, 21 Munros (peaks over 3,000 feet), miles of open forest and a fair number of deer and native critters that love to make the most of it all. There's plenty of space for wild camping but the most scenic lochside spots are popular – so popular, in fact, that a system of byelaws has recently been introduced to limit access.

Between March and September, campers in Loch Lomond and the Trossachs must now use a formal campsite or apply for a permit in the most popular lochside areas, which are known as Camping Management Zones. It's a frustrating situation for both campers and authorities but, as these areas account for just four per cent of the park, there are plenty of more secluded locations to head to instead. On the flipside, if you have your heart set on visiting this area during the summer months, it's worth considering the less wild options. There are several national park authority-managed campsites (see p.134), including Loch Chon and Loch Achray, providing a bookable almost wild experience with secluded pitches and toilets, but no showers.

Further north, The Cairngorms is Britain's biggest national park. This is the Highlands proper; home to 55 Munros and its biggest native forest. At 1,748 square miles, it's more than twice the size of the Lake District and yet it's visited by only a fraction of the number of visitors. You might say it's the wildest of the UK's national parks and, therefore, the wildest wild camping paradise.

If your idea of paradise, though, is beachside, not mountainside, there are still plenty of options in Scotland, both on the long coast of the mainland and its many islands, some of them blissfully remote. A few areas, like the Isle of Mull, have established wild camping zones as a way of managing pressure in spots that are particularly popular and have sensitive habitats that need protecting. If you arrive at any of these areas and there are already other campers, it is probably best to find an alternative place to stay. The best times to visit any popular spots are outside of school summer holidays and weekends.

DARTMOOR

Dartmoor National Park in Devon is a unique landscape of heather moorland, ancient stone circles, free-roaming ponies and, somewhere in among the thicket, a handful of hardy wild campers. Thanks to a series of byelaws, it's the only place in England where there's a legal right to wild camp without seeking landowner permission first. Wild camping or 'backpack camping', as it's named by the authorities in Dartmoor, is allowed only in certain areas and only as part of a walking expedition that involves carrying all your kit in a backpack. Visit dartmoor.gov.uk to find out exactly where pitching is permitted (alongside further information on how to camp on Dartmoor responsibly).

ELSEWHERE IN THE UK

The messaging around wild camping can be confusing. Many of the national park authorities in the UK state that wild camping without landowner permission is not legal and yet some of them still carry advice on their websites and leaflets about the practice. The reality is that wild camping is a tradition that has been going on for longer than the rules around it have existed. It is largely tolerated when done responsibly but the authorities cannot be seen to endorse or encourage it.

In upland areas of the Lake District, Snowdonia and the Brecon Beacons, if you camp responsibly on unenclosed ground above the highest fence line, your presence will likely go unchallenged. However, as was seen during the great camping rush of 2020, the tolerance of authorities and people living in these areas was tested by irresponsible actions of people camping outside of designated campsites. This makes it more important than ever to wild camp responsibly if we want to encourage acceptance of the wild camping community and continued rights in those areas where it's allowed.

Almost wild camping

For some, wild camping is a simple, uncomplicated pleasure. For others, it sounds appealing in theory but, in reality, when darkness begins to draw in, it all becomes a bit *Blair Witch Project*. The crack of a twig takes on as many decibels as a police siren and every stir of the wind makes it sound like somehow, somewhere, despite the two-day walk over mountains and the three-hour discussion over where's the most hidden spot to pitch, there's someone lurking metres away waiting to tell you you shouldn't be there. Don't worry. You're not alone. Or rather, you are alone. But you're not alone. If you know what we mean?

Wild camping is widely appealing in principle. But it's ever-so-slightly less widely appealing in practice. You want the isolation, the setting, the big view, the simplicity. But you also want the loo. And that unsettled feeling somewhere in your stomach (not the one regarding the loo). You fancy that gone too. Don't worry, if you're the wild-camping-but-rule-following type; that's where 'almost wild' comes in.

What do we mean by 'almost wild camping'?

Put simply, almost wild camping is staying on a designated campsite but emulating, as far as possible, the experience of wild camping by pitching in a remote location with very few facilities. It's popular because it allows you to enjoy many of the appealing things about true wild camping – the isolation, the peace and quiet, and the proximity to nature that comes from being off the grid – but, in some ways, it's also more accessible than wild camping, as it helps surmount common barriers, like feeling comfortable going to the loo and feeling safe and accounted for.

The primitive, almost wild campsites in this book are not aiming to replace or challenge wild camping as a practice. On the contrary, they're designed to make the outdoors and nature more accessible by accommodating people who wish to wild camp but recognise that it's not suited to their needs, such as having campfires, camping in large groups or staying for several nights at a time. For the uninitiated, these primitive campsites are also the perfect stepping stone on the route to true wild camping freedom.

TOP TIPS

▲ Check the facilities
There's no one-size-fits-all approach to the campsites in this book and no one-size-fits-all approach to the wilderness either. Check facilities ahead of time so you know what to expect. Some campsites don't have showers, others do, and a few might even have laundry facilities. Knowing what lies ahead will help you to pack appropriately.

▲ Stock up
Few campsites in this book will have an onsite shop and, in most cases, the best you're likely to get is a crumbling shed containing bags of firewood, boxes of eggs and a pile of yesterday's newspapers. Check the nearest shops before you leave – in some cases they're a boat journey or three-hour hike away – and bring adequate supplies for your stay.

▲ Cut the clutter
Camping is about being free and easy, so try not to pack the kitchen sink. Hikers have been packing all of their essential kit into a backpack for centuries, so the modern-day camper should be able to fit most things they need into one wheel barrow (which are commonly provided to help you get to your pitch). Remember, you can't park your car beside most pitches in this book.

▲ Book early
The downside to almost wild camping instead of the real thing is that you need to book a pitch (and pay for it). For the best spots, plan ahead and book early to avoid disappointment, particularly at the smallest campsites. Most locations among these pages can be booked online at coolcamping.com.

▲ Pitch perfect
Practise putting up your tent at home to remind yourself how to do it and check you have all the necessary parts. Use all the guy ropes available and insert pegs angled away from the tent at around 45 degrees. Keep your tent well-ventilated to avoid condensation building up inside. In blustery weather, pitch your tent so that the smallest end is facing into the wind, helping streamline it against the wind and keeping the rain out.

▲ Cook on the campfire
The great advantage of an almost wild campsite is the fact you can have a campfire, something that goes against the grain of the Leave No Trace ethos of genuine wild camping. So ditch the camping stove and get creative. Nothing compares to bangers skewer-cooked on the open flames or cooking fresh fish on a cast-iron skillet (see p.174).

▲ Slow down
Remember, part of the joy of both wild camping and almost wild camping is getting back to basics and really bedding yourself down in nature. So stop rushing and start relaxing. Switch off your mobile phone and learn to enjoy the slower pace of things. And leave time in your day's plans for simply being on the campsite and enjoying where you are.

Campsite locator

1	Wild Camping Cornwall	**31**	Gorfanc
2	Higher Pendeen	**32**	Gwalia Farm
3	Bush Farm	**33**	Smugglers Cove Boatyard
4	Bakesdown Farm	**34**	Graig Wen
5	Hole Station	**35**	North Rhinns
6	Woodland Edge	**36**	Marthrown of Mabie
7	Vallis Veg	**37**	Rue du Château
8	Abbey Home Organic Farm	**38**	Ruberslaw Wild Woods
9	Beech Estate	**39**	Blinkbonny Wood
10	Welsummer	**40**	Inchcailloch Wild Camping
11	Badgells Wood	**41**	Kintra Farm
12	Clifftop Camping	**42**	The Red Squirrel
13	Lee Valley Almost Wild Campsite	**43**	Ardnamurchan Campsite
14	Alderfen Marshes	**44**	Cleadale
15	The Norfolk Brickyard	**45**	Long Beach Campsite
16	Dreamy Hollow	**46**	Dall Cottage
17	Fire & Stars	**47**	Ace Hideaways
18	Farm on the Hill	**48**	Torridon Campsite
19	The Campsite	**49**	Badrallach
20	Piel Island	**50**	Lickisto Blackhouse
21	Turner Hall Farm	**51**	Cornish Yurt Holidays
22	Gill Head Farm	**52**	Wild Boar Wood
23	Hemscott Hill Farm	**53**	Lockhurst Hatch Farm
24	Into the Sticks	**54**	Gemini Camp
25	Dragonfly Woodland Camping	**55**	Little Seed Field
26	Cilrath Wood	**56**	Wanderlusts Gypsy Caravans
27	Digs in the Wig	**57**	Red Kite Tree Tents
28	Nantgwynfaen Organic Farm	**58**	Trellyn Woodland
29	Pytingwyn Lane	**59**	Ettrick Valley Yurts
30	Middle Ninfa Farm	**60**	Runach Arainn

Icon key

 Showers available

 Electric hook-up

 Waterside setting

 Toilets available

 Campfires allowed

 Near the sea

 Dogs allowed on site

 Woodland setting

 No. of pitches available

Campsites at a glance

IN THE WOODS

- **5** Hole Station
- **6** Woodland Edge
- **8** Abbey Home Organic Farm (the glade only)
- **9** Beech Estate
- **10** Welsummer
- **11** Badgells Wood
- **15** The Norfolk Brickyard
- **16** Dreamy Hollow
- **17** Fire & Stars
- **25** Dragonfly Woodland Camping
- **26** Cilrath Wood
- **27** Digs in the Wig
- **38** Ruberslaw Wild Woods
- **39** Blinkbonny Wood
- **47** Ace Hideaways

NEAR THE SEA

- **2** Higher Pendeen
- **12** Clifftop Camping
- **20** Piel Island
- **23** Hemscott Hill Farm
- **33** Smugglers Cove Boatyard
- **34** Graig Wen
- **35** North Rhinns
- **41** Kintra Farm
- **43** Ardnamurchan Campsite
- **44** Cleadale
- **45** Long Beach Campsite
- **48** Torridon Campsite
- **49** Badrallach
- **50** Lickisto Blackhouse

BESIDE A RIVER

- **29** Pytingwyn Lane
- **31** Gorfanc
- **33** Smugglers Cove Boatyard
- **34** Graig Wen
- **37** Rue du Château
- **42** The Red Squirrel
- **46** Dall Cottage
- **47** Ace Hideaways

IN THE MOUNTAINS

- **18** Farm on the Hill
- **19** The Campsite
- **21** Turner Hall Farm
- **22** Gill Head Farm
- **30** Middle Ninfa Farm
- **32** Gwalia Farm
- **33** Smugglers Cove Boatyard
- **34** Graig Wen
- **40** Inchcailloch Wild Camping
- **42** The Red Squirrel
- **44** Cleadale
- **45** Long Beach Campsite
- **46** Dall Cottage
- **48** Torridon Campsite
- **49** Badrallach

SHORT WALK TO THE PUB

- **2** Higher Pendeen
- **7** Vallis Veg
- **9** Beech Estate
- **10** Welsummer
- **12** Clifftop Camping
- **13** Lee Valley Almost Wild Campsite
- **14** Alderfen Marshes
- **17** Fire & Stars
- **20** Piel Island
- **21** Turner Hall Farm
- **25** Dragonfly Woodland Camping
- **36** Marthrown of Mabie
- **42** The Red Squirrel
- **45** Long Beach Campsite

CAMPFIRES ALLOWED

Every campsite featured permits controlled campfires, apart from **20**, **21**, **43** and **44**.

OPEN ALL YEAR

- **3** Bush Farm
- **5** Hole Station
- **8** Abbey Home Organic Farm
- **12** Clifftop Camping

17 Fire & Stars
18 Farm on the Hill
19 The Campsite
20 Piel Island
24 Into the Sticks
28 Nantgwynfaen Organic Farm
30 Middle Ninfa Farm
31 Gorfanc
32 Gwalia Farm
34 Graig Wen
35 North Rhinns
36 Marthrown of Mabie
42 The Red Squirrel
45 Long Beach Campsite
48 Torridon Campsite
49 Badrallach

'GLAMPING' OPTION

1 Wild Camping Cornwall
2 Higher Pendeen
4 Bakesdown Farm
8 Abbey Home Organic Farm
9 Beech Estate
10 Welsummer
15 The Norfolk Brickyard
22 Gill Head Farm
24 Into the Sticks
28 Nantgwynfaen Organic Farm
33 Smugglers Cove Boatyard
34 Graig Wen
35 North Rhinns
36 Marthrown of Mabie
38 Ruberslaw Wild Woods
47 Ace Hideaways
50 Lickisto Blackhouse

DOGS ALLOWED

3 Bush Farm
6 Woodland Edge
10 Welsummer
11 Badgells Wood
13 Lee Valley Almost Wild Campsite
16 Dreamy Hollow
17 Fire & Stars
20 Piel Island
21 Turner Hall Farm

22 Gill Head Farm
23 Hemscott Hill Farm
27 Digs in the Wig
28 Nantgwynfaen Organic Farm
29 Pytingwyn Lane
31 Gorfanc
32 Gwalia Farm
33 Smugglers Cove Boatyard
34 Graig Wen
35 North Rhinns
36 Marthrown of Mabie
37 Rue du Château
38 Ruberslaw Wild Woods
39 Blinkbonny Wood
41 Kintra Farm
42 The Red Squirrel
43 Ardnamurchan Campsite
45 Long Beach Campsite
46 Dall Cottage
47 Ace Hideaways
48 Torridon Campsite
49 Badrallach
50 Lickisto Blackhouse

ADULTS ONLY

5 Hole Station
13 Lee Valley Almost Wild Campsite (over 12s)
32 Gwalia Farm

PARK BESIDE YOUR PITCH

3 Bush Farm
4 Bakesdown Farm
12 Clifftop Camping
15 The Norfolk Brickyard
19 The Campsite
21 Turner Hall Farm
22 Gill Head Farm
23 Hemscott Hill Farm
25 Dragonfly Woodland Camping
29 Pytingwyn Lane
41 Kintra Farm
43 Ardnamurchan Campsite
46 Dall Cottage (if you have a 4x4)
48 Torridon Campsite
49 Badrallach

ENGLAND

1

Wild Camping Cornwall

Celtic fire festivals used to be held at Bartinney Castle, dedicated to the sun god Belenos. They seem to have worked. Cornwall's Penwith Peninsula is one of the sunniest spots on the British Isles and today, half a mile down a footpath from the castle's faintest of earth remains, there's a tiny wild campsite well placed to enjoy it.

There are just a couple of pitches and a pre-erected bell tent at Wild Camping Cornwall, which opened in 2021 after moving from another temporary location nearer the coast. The new site has been planted with dozens of trees that will make for quite the hideaway in years to come. For the time being it's best to hope Belenos keeps the wind gods at bay, since the place can feel a little exposed when it gets gusty.

Facilities consist of a composting loo, a gas-powered shower and a firepit at each pitch (a bag of logs comes with every booking), and the stars are excellent night lights. The nearest neighbours here are a nature reserve and a string of Iron Age humps and bumps of significance, cared for by English Heritage, so light pollution is non-existent.

There's more to the location, of course, than hiking through history. There's a beach within 10–15 minutes' drive in almost every direction you choose. Sennen Cove (six miles) is Cornwall's most westerly surfing hotspot and frequently tops lists of the UK's best beaches, while lesser-known spots like Lamorna Cove, St Loy's Cove and Penberth offer smaller nooks where you can enjoy rock pooling under jagged cliffs.

Higher Trevarthen, Grumbla, Penzance, Cornwall TR20 8QY ● 07842 888645
contact@wildcampingcornwall.co.uk ● wildcampingcornwall.co.uk

Open July and August.
OS Explorer map 102 (SW 402 295).
Nearest pub The nearest options are all in St Just, two miles away, where The Star Inn (01736 788767), The Wellington Hotel (wellingtonhotelcornwall.co.uk; 01736 787319) and The Kings Arms (01736 788545) are all just off the main square.
Access There's a parking area at the site entrance, then it's a 20–100-yard walk to the pitches. The owners can help move your stuff in their truck on Mondays and Fridays.
Mobile phone signal Better than nothing.
If it's full There's another back-to-basics camping meadow at Ryn Gwari Farm (07786 512985) near St Just, while the football club at Mousehole turns the training area and grassland around its pitches into a temporary campsite each summer (mouseholecamping.co.uk; 07470 920006).

2

Higher Pendeen

There's a certain irony to the fact that the last thing you pass before reaching Higher Pendeen Camping is a busy holiday park. By the seaside, five miles north of Newquay, there's no denying that this is prime tourist territory, so it's all the more delightful to discover this tiny, slightly sloping, five-pitch camping meadow shoehorned into the Menalhyl Valley.

The Sterling family has been working Gluvian Farm for four generations but it's only recently that Liz and Mike have opened this pocket-sized site to campers. There's a composting toilet, an open-air shower and a drinking water tap but little else. Fresh farm veg is often available – particularly in late summer – and Liz seems to know half the local fishing fleet if you want fresh seafood.

Higher Pendeen's campsite app recommending local attractions is undoubtedly the most high-tech feature you'll find at any campsite in this book, though it's little use without the mobile phone signal needed to download it. All you really need to know, however, is that it takes around 10 minutes to walk to Mawgan Porth beach through the farm. From there you can follow the South West Coast Path to Newquay or trek north on a day-long walk to Padstow along a stretch of the north Cornwall coast that takes in some of the most spectacular sea stacks along the trail.

Gluvian Farm, Mawgan Porth, Newquay, Cornwall TR8 4BG
higherpendeen@gmail.com • higherpendeencamping.com

Open March–October.
OS Explorer map 106 (SW 858 668).
Nearest pub The Merrymoor Inn (merrymoorinn.com; 01637 860258) in Mawgan Porth is a 15-minute walk from the campsite and overlooks the beach.
Access Good road access then little more than a 25-yard walk from where you park to the camping meadow.
Mobile phone signal If you're on Three or EE you've got a good chance (try standing at the top of the meadow and waving your arms around like you long to be struck by lightning). Vodafone is patchy and this is total wilderness if you're with O2.
If it's full It's five miles to family-friendly Trewan Hall (trewan-hall.co.uk; 01637 880261) but that takes you inland. If you'd prefer to stay on the coast, head a little south and try family-friendly Porth Joke Campsite (crantockholiday.co.uk; 01637 831207), nine miles away and also within walking distance of the sea.

3

Bush Farm

Don't be fooled by the rather industrial approach to Bush Farm campsite. You may arrive via the old farmyard, now home to a commercial vehicle training centre and the campsite reception, but you're soon let loose on 200 acres of Cornish countryside. A map of the site will help wild camping enthusiasts navigate their way straight past the main camping meadow (a handful of pitches for people who like to be near the facilities) and out on to rough tracks across the farm.

Bush Farm was given over to a rewilding project in 2020, which included the planting of 100 acres of wildflower meadows. It seems appropriate, then, that campers are being given the chance to rewild here too. There are countless places to pitch a tent, from hillside spots with countryside views to secluded wooded and riverside areas. It's yours to explore. If you can get there, you can camp there – just make sure you leave 50 yards between you and the nearest neighbour.

Off-road driving to find your pitch gives the place an almost safari atmosphere that's a far cry from the many holiday park-style campsites on the Cornish coast. But most people do head to this part of the world for the beaches. If water's a draw, the River Lynher runs through the site – perfect for a splashabout in hot weather – and if it's the seaside you're after, it's 15 miles to the beach at Whitsand Bay and the harbour town of Looe.

Pillaton, Saltash, Cornwall PL12 6QY ● 07875 557160
bushfarmcampsite@outlook.com ● bushfarmcampsite.co.uk

Open All year.
OS Explorer map 108 (SX 378 621).
Nearest pub Nothing within strolling distance. It's two miles to the Weary Friar Inn in Pillarton (wearyfriar.co.uk; 01579 350238), a popular, food-orientated pub, originally built for the stonemasons working on the 12th-century church next door.
Access You can drive around the farm on farm tracks and the most popular places to pitch are accessible by car.
Mobile phone signal Good coverage on all networks.
If it's full Resort to the main meadow if the wild camping pitches are gone. Otherwise, Kinrowan Park (kinrowanparkholidays.co.uk; 01503 241252; eight miles) is a touring park but has a few secluded camping pitches, while Cockles Farm (cocklesfarm.com; 01752 473706) has just opened a campsite on the edge of Saltash, five miles away.

4

Bakesdown Farm

"Which meadow would you like?" That's often the first question when you try to book a pitch at Bakesdown Farm, 10 minutes' drive from Widemouth Bay on the North Cornwall coast. And they don't mean 'the family meadow' or 'the busy one by the bogs'. They mean which meadow would you like to be yours? There are at least two fields between each camping space at Bakesdown, with the wildest spots a good 200-yard walk from the main farmyard. Not only do you have these entire meadows to yourself, but also private use of the compost toilet and the gas-heated shower in each.

Someone on the farm was recently introduced to a lawnmower and has trimmed out neat spots where you can pitch. Most of the place, however, is covered in knee-high grass pimpled with buttercups, and no such introductions have been made to the hedgetrimmer. The farm is an eclectic world of spreading shrubbery and sprawling bramble bushes that sag under the weight of thumb-sized blackberries in September. It's a great stomping ground for active kids.

Nearby Widemouth Bay is a bit of a surfing hub and there are numerous schools and board rental companies if you want to give it a try. It's also a good place to pick up the coastal path and take in the sea views from terra firma – the tough but rewarding route to Crackington Haven is well known for the abundance of butterflies in Chipman Valley and the countless little waterfalls along the way, and there's a handy bus back when you reach the end.

Lower Bakesdown Farm, Marhamchurch, Bude, Cornwall EX23 0HJ ● 07958 543118
bakesdownfarmcamping@gmail.com ● bakesdownfarm.co.uk

Open April–October.
OS Explorer map 111 (SS 246 007).
Nearest pub Nothing within walking distance. The family-run Old Orchard Inn in Week St Mary (01288 341646) is the closest at two miles, but there are more options if you head to the coast, notably in Widemouth Bay and Bude.
Access Car access to some pitches or a maximum walk of around 200 yards.
Mobile phone signal Phone signal is the stuff of fiction around here.
If it's full There are two good campsites just outside of Bude – Cerenety (cerenetycampsite.co.uk; 07380 940849) and Atlantic Farm (atlanticsurfpods.co.uk; 01288 355288). The latter also has glamping options, including a treehouse.

5

Hole Station

Situated on the land of a former railway station, this wooded campsite has 18 camping pitches across some 23 acres, each with a tarp kitchen shelter strung up to one side. Owners Greg and Liz live in what was once the old ticket office and, together with their family, have dedicated the last decade or so to slowly bringing the wood back to its former glory, by coppicing and pollarding through the winter months.

While the pitches are well spread among the wood, ensuring plenty of privacy, the over-18s policy also ensures the place is far quieter than most campsites in Devon and, if you request one of the pitches furthest from the parking area, you'll find yourself well out of earshot of others. A noisy woodpecker is perhaps the most likely culprit of an early-morning wake-up call. Squirrels, on the other hand, have the habit of being near-silent, so it's best to make sure you always seal away your food.

With the railway gone, some of its path now forms a cycle route to nearby Hatherleigh, which can be linked up with the popular Tarka Trail for a car-free, off-road option. The young River Torridge also passes within a mile or so of the campsite, with a few access points for wild swimmers along its banks. There's a deep pool below the bridge in the village of Sheepwash (three miles) that's particularly good for a proper plunge, with a pub just up the lane for warming up afterwards (The Half Moon Inn; halfmoonsheepwash.co.uk; 01409 231376).

Highampton, Beaworthy, Devon EX21 5JH ● 01409 231266
holestation@fastmail.fm ● holestationcampsite.co.uk

Open All year.
OS Explorer map 112 (SS 466 034).
Nearest pub The Golden Inn in Highampton (01409 231200) and the Black River Inn in Black Torrington (blackriverinn.co.uk; 01409 231888) are both just under a mile and a half from the campsite.
Access There's no car access to the woods and the walking distance varies depending on your pitch choice (from a few yards to 200). Wheelbarrows are provided.
Mobile phone signal Patchy but reliably at least 3G for those on EE and O2.
If it's full It's a 20-minute drive to Hideaway Camping (hideawaycamping.co.uk; 01837 871777), rustic and quirky and with a couple of glamping options, or try to bag one of the handful of pitches above the vines at rightfully popular Ten Acres Vineyard (tenacresvineyardcamping.co.uk; 01837 83892).

With the railway gone, some of its path now
forms a cycle route to nearby Hatherleigh, which
can be linked up with the popular Tarka Trail for
a car-free, off-road option.

6

Woodland Edge

Opened in 2020, this three-acre patch of woodland, under Forestry Commission Stewardship, is particularly popular for hammock camping, with native ash, wild cherry and oak trees seemingly planted the perfect distance apart. Owner Simon is an enthusiastic hammock camper himself and can rent you one if needed. Or you can go hunting for a patch of ground without too many roots on which to pitch your tent.

There's not much to the place, which is really what makes it so special. Facilities consist of nothing more than a composting loo and you'll need to bring your own water, but there's a campfire pit provided and, though logs are available to buy, you're welcome to forage for fallen timber if you like.

It's a 10-minute drive north to the villages of Lovington or West Lydford, where there's access to the River Brue for wild swimming (with a weir and rope swing at the latter), while Haynes International Motor Museum (himm.co.uk; 01963 440804) is the nearest attraction (it's only a mile as the crow flies, though a cumbersome route makes it a very long walk or a five-minute drive). It's a half hour, meanwhile, to Glastonbury Tor, and the same to similar but far quieter Burrow Mump, a 24-metre-high hill topped by the ruins of St Michael's church.

Strawberry Lane, Yeovil, Somerset BA22 7LR • 07586 350862
woodlandedge20@gmail.com

Open March–October.
OS Explorer map 129 (ST 605 285).
Nearest pub It's just under two miles to The Sparkford Inn (sparkfordinnpubyeovil.co.uk; 01963 440218); there's not a particularly handy footpath if you're walking but the road is nice and quiet. With its beams, flagstone floors and generally cosy 14th-century character, the family-friendly Red Lion (redlionbabcary.co.uk; 01458 223230), four miles away in Babcary, is worth the extra distance.
Access There's room for up to five or six cars by the grassy, gated entrance to the wood. Then walk into the woods as far as you like.
Mobile phone signal Reliable 4G on most networks.
If it's full Orchard Farm (orchardfarmcampsite.co.uk; 01458 851107; eight miles), is less wild and woody but it welcomes tents and there are still plenty of trees. If you're after more comforts, the site is within walking distance of Woodland Escape Glamping (woodlandescape.co.uk; 01225 290924).

7

Vallis Veg

Just yards off the East Mendip Way footpath, 15 or so camping pitches are dispersed among young tree plantations at this small-scale vegetable farm, one mile west of Frome. Pitches are less wild than they initially seem – most have been flattened out and wood chippings have been laid to improve drainage and stability – but there's no hot water and showers come in the form of a wood hut with a bucket.

Though three or four pitches are available in an open meadow, most open spaces on the farm are striped with leafy produce growing in jumbled lines, and polytunnels brimming with tomatoes in camping season. Excess produce is occasionally sold to campers and it takes less than half an hour to walk into the centre of Frome for further food and conveniences.

Stroll the East Mendip Way in the opposite direction, meanwhile, for a serene trail beside Egford Brook and the River Mells. When you reach the village of Great Elm, a mile along the path, you can cross the old ford and take a scenic detour to a huge but little-known 19th-century ironworks. Now ruined, it comes complete with workers' houses, crumbled pumping stations and the old weir, all now hugged by moss and ivy and wonderfully atmospheric.

Vallis Veg, Egford, Frome, Somerset BA11 3JQ ● 07870 704299
camping@vallisveg.co.uk ● *vallisveg.co.uk*

Open May–October.
OS Explorer map 142 (ST 758 488).
Nearest pub The Royal Oak (01373 463520; impressive range of ciders and real ales) is less than a mile away on the western edge of Frome, reached via a quiet country lane. Or follow the East Mendip Way into the centre of town, where more options include The Griffin (griffinfrome.com; 01373 301251; often has live music), The Three Swans (threeswans.net; 01488 682721) and The Lamb and Fountain (01373 463414).
Access There's a £9 'climate charge' if you're coming by car (parking just off the entrance track then a 50–200-yard walk to most pitches). It's a 40-minute walk or 20-minute cycle to Frome train station (just under two miles away).
Mobile phone signal Reliable 4G on all networks.
If it's full Try low-key and family-friendly Botany Farm (botanycamping.com; 07713 404233), near Warminster, nine miles away.

...most open spaces on the farm are striped with leafy produce growing in jumbled lines, and polytunnels brimming with tomatoes in camping season.

8

Abbey Home Organic Farm

Ask owner Hilary about her wild camping site and she'll probably start telling you about the farm's grassy 'Green Field Camping', with composting toilets, bucket showers you can heat with your campfire, and far-reaching views across the Cotswolds countryside. But lean in. Explain what you're *really* looking for and Hilary might just tell you about the magical glade.

A full mile from the rest of the campsite, the magical glade is an exclusive hire spot in the woods with space for about three small tents or a handful of hammocks. Since the wood was only planted 20 years ago, the trees are still relatively small, giving campers the best of both worlds: sheltered seclusion and warming dappled sunlight. If you want back-to-basics tomfoolery, the Green Field is still great for sociable campers but, with a campfire to yourself and an inspiring dawn chorus, the glade will always be the true wild campers' choice.

The benefit of occupying such a secluded spot on what is, really, a more established campsite, is a decent host of facilities if you walk the mile back to the main farm hub. There's a café, an abundantly stocked farm shop and farm tours and various courses throughout the year run by Hilary and family. It's two miles, meanwhile, into the centre of Cirencester for all other amenities.

Burford Road, Cirencester, Gloucestershire GL7 5HF ● 01285 640441
theorganicfarmshop.co.uk

Open All Year.
OS Explorer map 169 (SP 043 036).
Nearest pub The farm's own shop and café has plenty to feed you but, for a pint, there's no pub within easy strolling distance. The many options of Cirencester are within two or three miles, while The Village Pub (barnsleyhouse.com; 01285 740421) – yes, it's actually called that – is three miles away in Barnsley.
Access The green field is car-free but you can park right at the entrance to the meadow. The magical glade has parking around 100 yards from the pitching space.
Mobile phone signal 4G for most folks in the green field but much patchier in the magical glade.
If it's full It's not far to Far Peak Camping (farpeakcamping.co.uk; 01285 700370) in the very middle of the Cotswolds AONB but it can be busy in the summer. Rouselands Farm (rouselandsfarmcampsite.co.uk; 01666 510315), 15 miles south, is a quieter option.

*Explain what you're really looking for
and Hilary might just tell you about the
magical glade, an exclusive hire spot
a mile from the rest of the campsite.*

9

Beech Estate

If you're not already excited about camping at Beech Estate, the drive into this Sussex wood will help build anticipation. Slow down and open the car windows for a whiff of pine, the sound of birds and, perhaps, the sight of woodland creatures scampering off into the trees. All this before you even reach the car park. From there, it's a walk of between 100 and 300 yards to the nearest pitches. There are around 30 in total, all off grid and with a firepit dug into the ground. The site does also have bell tents and a camping meadow but the vast treescape ensures it never feels crowded, with everything tucked among the greenery on the edge of a 600-acre wood.

Spring is perhaps the best time to camp at the estate. Bluebells are in full bloom and positively carpet the place, and only the hardier, early-season campers are in attendance. For the wildest pitches, choose a 'Faraway'. You'll have to walk further but the seclusion, right in the heart of the wood, is worth it and there's still a clearing with compost loos and basic bucket showers nearby. A few tucked-away pitches are designated for hammock campers too (just state if you want one on booking).

There's no real reason to use your car. Three pubs lie within walking distance – mostly through the woods and then out on public footpaths – and den building is so encouraged here that the campsite has an online guide to it. If you do want to venture further afield, however, you're well placed in 1066 country – historic Battle is a couple of miles down the road, with the south coast at Hastings a few miles beyond.

Kane Hythe Road, Battle, East Sussex TN33 9QU ● 01273 980218
info@pegsandpitches.co.uk ● pegsandpitches.co.uk

Open April–November.
OS Explorer map 124 (TQ 715 169).
Nearest pub There are three pubs you can walk to from Beech Estate, mostly on off-road routes through the estate's private woodland: The Squirrel Inn (thesquirrelinn-battle.co.uk; 01424 772717), The White Hart (white-hart-netherfield.co.uk; 01424 817848) and the Netherfield Arms (netherfieldarms.co.uk; 01424 838282).
Access There's a designated car park, then pitches are 100–300 yards away.
Mobile phone signal It's patchier than a pirate but best on EE and O2.
If it's full Try the small camping paddock at Dogwood Cottage (dogwoodcamping.co.uk; 01424 883570), 11 miles to the east, or larger Buckhurst Campsite (buckhurstcamping. com; 07517 477447) a couple of miles north of Hastings.

10

Welsummer

If you want a campsite that's got a wild side, choose a site with an owner who has one too. Laura, who runs Welsummer with partner Med, used to camp in the woods here as a child, pegging out a tarp among the trees, long before the place had the facilities on offer today. The campsite is situated on her family's smallholding and these days there are loos, showers and a washing-up area – but they've not gone too fancy. With a rainwater harvesting system and a wood-burning stove for hot water, it's stylish but rustic. It's a description that works for the rest of the site too.

Campers with their own tents can choose to book pitches in the woods or the meadow, with the woodland pitches offering a wilder ambience. It's best to discuss your tent size when booking, since these more secluded pitches vary in size. The site has some glamping options, too, in the shape of four bell tents and a converted hay bale trailer, but Welsummer is small enough and everything's spread out enough that you can feel nicely isolated when you want to, particularly come nightfall when all falls quiet and the campfire is crackling.

Above all else it's the laid-back, friendliness of Laura and Med that really make the place, and the site is as accommodating to kids as to couples. There's a little onsite shop selling smallholding produce, hot drinks and snacks, and there's a 15th-century pub a short cross-country walk away. The Kent countryside is yours to explore and the South Coast is a half-hour drive.

Address: Chalk House, Lenham Road, Kent ME17 1NQ ● 07850 464338
bookapitchatwelsummer@gmail.com ● welsummercamping.com

Open April–October.
OS Explorer map 137 (TQ 866 505).
Nearest pub The whitewashed, 15th-century Pepperbox Inn (thepepperboxinn.co.uk; 01622 842558) is less than a mile away and can be reached by a cross-country route on local footpaths. It has a large garden terrace, open fires and a good menu.
Access Cars are parked away from the camping area. To reach the woodland pitches, it's a walk of 30–60 yards. Wheelbarrows are available.
Mobile phone signal Generally reliable 4G on all networks.
If it's full It's two miles to Plumtree Caravan Park (plumtreeparkcampingandcaravan. com) but we'd go the extra distance – seven miles – to unpretentious and campfire-friendly Palace Farm (palacefarm.com; 01795 886365).

Laura, who runs Welsummer with partner Med, used to camp in the woods here as a child, pegging out a tarp among the trees...

11

Badgells Wood

Finding Badgells Wood Campsite is all part of the fun since, confusingly, the wood itself is called White Horse Wood and it's only the campsite that has a different name. Throw in a handful of narrow, unsigned rural lanes and there are inevitably a few more wrong turns before you reach the track (a tarmac relic from former use as a World War II training area) and a couple of temporary buildings that make up Badgells' reception block.

Beyond lie 250 acres of native woodland sat atop a shelf in the north of the Kent Downs. Around one eighth of this has been set aside for campers, which may not sound like much, but leave your car and trundle off into the trees and you quickly realise the space on offer is endless.

Inevitably, the wildest rewards come from walking as far as possible from reception and civilization, though thankfully, composting toilets dotted around the place mean you needn't walk as far to the loo. Old huts and trenches leave intriguing reminders of the wood's former uses and, when you do spill back out into the open, you're rewarded with far-reaching views across the Medway Valley and the Pilgrims' Way footpath running along the perimeter of the trees.

Whitehorse Road, Meopham, Kent DA13 0UF • 07528 609324
enquiries@badgellswoodcamping.co.uk • badgellswoodcamping.co.uk

Open Easter–October.
OS Explorer map 148 (TQ 663 621).
Nearest pub The Amazon & Tiger (01474 814705) in Harvel is the nearest pub (just over a mile) but, though a bit further away, the road-free walk out of the south of the woods and along footpaths to Birling makes The Nevill Bull (nevillbullbirling.com; 01732 849045) just as appealing.
Access There are a handful of pitches near the main track at the entrance, with one or two for motorhomes, so you needn't walk far from your car if you don't want to. But for the wilder pitches its best to head right to the back of the woods away from others. Wheelbarrows are provided.
Mobile phone signal Generally good but it varies depending on how deep into the woods you go.
If it's full It's a half-hour drive to Welsummer (see p.52) for another woodland option and only a little further to Palace Farm (palacefarm.com; 01795 886365).

12

Clifftop Camping

What could be wilder than camping on the edge of an enormous estuary island, about a quarter of which is a national nature reserve? In fact, the Isle of Sheppey, at the mouth of the River Thames, is pimpled with almost a dozen different caravan parks, which scatter like barnacles across the island's north-eastern rump. But among them, in a great hundred-acre apron of green space, is low-key Connetts Farm, home to a pleasingly more unkempt kind of campsite.

There are several different camping areas on the farm, though in total there are rarely more than 15 or 20 pitches. As the name suggests, the most spectacular spots are along the clifftop, looking out across a wind-turbine-studded estuary with Essex in the very distance. On a clear day you can see the silhouettes of Red Sands Fort too – a set of abandoned World War II sea defences that sit on stilts six miles off the shore.

While the clifftops afford the best views, those on the hunt for that more isolated feel can turn to the pondside pitches (there's a boat you can hop into) or explore a small wood (good for hammocks or tying up a tarp for extra shelter). Every area shares the same central set of composting toilets and water taps and there are no showers. Access to the beach involves an undignified scramble down the shallow cliff face but it's practically private on the sands below.

Connetts Farm, Eastchurch, Isle of Sheppey, Kent ME12 4JL ● 07453 639230
clifftopcamping@gmail.com ● clifftopcamping.co.uk

Open All Year.
OS Explorer map 149 (TQ 987 729).
Nearest pub The big holiday parks either side of the campsite (about a quarter of a mile in each direction) both have what claim to be pubs on the premises, in among the statics, but for a 'proper' pub, The Castle Inn (01795 880571), a smidgen over a mile away in Eastchurch, is the closest.
Access You can park beside most pitches in the open clifftop meadow but, in most cases, car parking is in the farmyard, then it's up to a 200-yard walk to your spot.
Mobile phone signal Not as good as you'd expect in such an open clifftop location. Best with Three and EE but it feels like wilderness if you're with Vodafone.
If it's full There are dozens of caravan parks all along the Sheppey coast, many of which welcome tents. But for a less commercial camping experience, try 5 Acres (5acc.co.uk) five miles from the bridge on to Sheppey.

13

Lee Valley Almost Wild Campsite

"No collusion!", as a former American president once said. You'd have thought the founders of this campsite might have pre-arranged its name in order to shoehorn their way into this guidebook. And, when you find the campsite on the map – half a mile from a train station, five miles from the M25 and less than 20 miles from central London – you'd be right to question, how wild can it really be?

The answer, however, is surprising. With no showers, just 15 pitches and the vast majority of campers who come here arriving by bicycle or even by canoe, this parcel of partially wooded land, where the River Lee intercepts the Lee Canal, is as wild as you're ever likely to imagine this close to the capital.

Around 10 of the pitches are in a communal meadow space and, since the campsite is only open on weekends, it's not possible to camp here on a quiet mid-week day when you'll have it all to yourself. Book one of the five woodland pitches, however, and there's a genuine feel of isolation, with bats and owls as potential company and your campfire filling the leafy surroundings with its glow.

Fishing (with a licence) is permitted and, if you haven't paddled here in your own canoe (a good day-long paddle from London each way), you can hire one from Lee Valley Canoe Cycle (lvcc.link; 01992 676650) just over the road from the campsite.

Nazeing New Road, Broxbourne, Hertfordshire EN10 6TD ● 03000 030619
almostwild@leevalleypark.org.uk ● visitleevalley.org.uk

Open Weekends from April–October.
OS Explorer map 174 (TL 377 068).
Nearest pub It takes less than 10 minutes to cross the road, go through a car park and along the canal-side to The Crown (vintageinn.co.uk; 01992 462244), which is popular with boaters and has picnic benches along the waterside.
Access There's a limited amount of parking at the campsite entrance (a code for the gate is issued when you book) and from there it's a short walk to your pitch, but many people come here by bike or walk from the station (around 20 minutes) so parking spaces are never an issue.
Mobile phone signal Wild or not, this campsite is on the edge of town and within cycling distance of London, so the mobile phone signal is excellent.
If it's full The Lee Valley Park Authority run another more established campsite further down river, just within the boundaries of the M25 (visitleevalley.org.uk; 02085 295689).

...half a mile from a train station, five miles from the M25 and less than 20 miles from central London – you'd be right to question, how wild can it really be?

14

Alderfen Marshes

On the edge of Mid-Yare National Nature Reserve and a Site of Special Scientific Interest, Alderfen Marshes limits campers to a maximum of three nights to minimise their impact. So you'll even get the authentic wild camping experience of being moved on if you've outstayed your welcome. And most people do wish they could stay for longer. There are no showers and drinking water is brought to the site in tanks but, with just four of five pitches pocketed away among blackberry bushes and young willow trees, it offers true escapism for the wild at heart.

Water is at the centre of the Alderfen camping experience. The River Yare shapes the land here, meandering its way through Norwich, seven miles west of the campsite, and spreading its watery fingers as it flows east to create hidden channels and reedy streams all along the river banks. Almost every pitch at Alderfen is on the waterside in some form (though pitches have a tendency to move around) and, to ensure no camper misses out, your camping fee includes the hire of a Canadian canoe. As a result, paddling on the Yare and exploring Bargate Broad will become your day's activities (there's a good pub within watery reach; see below), while the Wherryman's Way footpath is also on the doorstep.

Alderfen, Common Road, Surlingham, Norwich, Norfolk NR14 7AW ● 07788 154755
info@go-moco.co.uk ● go-moco.co.uk

Open Mid May–September.
OS Explorer map OL40 (TG 316 072).
Nearest pub Coldham Hall (coldhamhall.com; 01508 538366) and The Ferry House (surlinghamferry.co.uk; 01508 538659) are both riverside and both 10–15 minutes' stroll away, but why walk when you can canoe? The former is easy to reach by river, paddling through the narrow waterways by the campsite, then out on to Bargate, a 18-acre broad that's home to the ruins of old sailing wherries, before following a final channel to the pub, which has a waterside deck where you can while away the hours.
Access No parking by your pitch but trolleys are provided for the 100-yard walk.
Mobile phone signal Expect to walk around waving your arms in the air like you're at a 90s pop concert but, in the right places, there's plenty of coverage.
If it's full Family-friendly Whitlingham Broad Campsite (whitlinghambroadcampsite.com; 07794 401591; seven miles) has a good location within walking distance of Norwich and also has broads access for canoeing.

15

The Norfolk Brickyard

The last bricks were fired on the Holkham Estate in 1951 and the old brickyard, after more than 200 years of use, fell into disrepair. It wasn't until half a century later, when owners Tim and Catherine had their wedding in an old barn there, that it was truly rediscovered. As friends raved about their night camping in the wilderness the couple struck upon the idea of opening a campsite. And today, the ivy-clad brickworks, under a gingham cloth of moss and greenery, has become the centrepiece of Norfolk Brickyard Campsite.

At its heart, the brickyard is a family site. You can park by most pitches, hire bikes, use the homemade pizza oven and there are even a couple of safari tents for glampers. But head for one of the secluded spots deep in the woods, like 'Keepers Camp', and it feels like you have the place entirely to yourself. Toilets are of the composting kind and showers come in the form of a metal bucket you can heat over your campfire, before winching into a tree (though, whether by coincidence or by coronavirus, a 'proper' shower was also added in 2020).

Holkham Hall, Holkham Bay and Burnham Overy Staithe make for spectacular walks no matter the time of year. Arguably, the best experiences here are had well outside of the usual camping season, when thousands of pink-footed geese overwinter on the local marshes and flood the skies at dawn and dusk; the campsite is all but empty, the pubs are quieter and bucket showers have some added almost-wild frisson.

Burnham Road, Peterstone, Wells-next-the-Sea, Norfolk NR23 1RR ● 01328 730663
tim@norfolkbrickyard.co.uk ● **norfolkbrickyard.co.uk**

Open All year.
OS Explorer map 251 (TF 862 427).
Nearest pub There's a small clutch of pubs and cafés in Burnham Market (a little under two miles away and with a reputation for being on the pricey side), while The Hero (theheroburnhamovery.co.uk; 01328 738334) in Burnham Overy Staithe is not quite harbourside but it's only a matter of yards and none the worse for it.
Access Parking at most pitches, though some deeper in the woods require a short walk.
Mobile phone signal Good, but if you're with EE you'll have to hunt for a bit.
If it's full In August, try the view-tastic pop-up campsite on the hill behind Burnham Overy Staithe (Burnham Breck Camping; burnhambreck.co.uk; two miles). The rest of the year, try popular Deepdale Farm (deepdalefarm.co.uk; 01485 210256; four miles).

The last bricks were fired on the Holkham Estate
in 1951 and the old brickyard, after more than
200 years of use, fell into disrepair.

16

Dreamy Hollow

The green furrows that run through Dreamy Hollow Campsite were thought to be old drainage ditches before a recent survey revealed they were, in fact, a three-and-a-half acre network of First World War training trenches snaking through the woods. Thought to have been dug in 1915, they've now undergone extensive restorations and add yet more intrigue to a campsite that's already a patchwork of dips and hollows, clearings and trees.

There are fewer than 20 pitches in total, some in pairs – great for groups to book – others tucked further into the wood or in an elevated position on the edge of the trees, with views across the North Norfolk countryside. 'Wills' is the ideal size for hammocks, while 'Nigel's Nook' is always the earliest pitch to get booked out, flanked by high banks of ferns and a real sun trap in summer.

The sea-sculpted curvature of Norfolk's hump means there's around 20 miles of coastline arching equidistantly around the campsite. It's a 15-minute drive to Heacham Beach to the west, Brancaster Beach to the north and several others in between, while some of the most scenic stretches of the Norfolk Coastal Path, taking in Holme Dunes and marshy Thornham Harbour, are popular with budding birders, whatever the season.

Fakenham Road, Stanhoe, Kings Lynn, Norfolk PE31 8PX ● 07564 226780
office@dreamyhollowcamping.co.uk ● dreamyhollowcamping.co.uk

Open Easter–October.
OS Explorer map 250 (TF 797 345).
Nearest pub It's two miles to the foodie, gastro-style Duck Inn in Stanhoe (duckinn.co.uk; 01485 518330) and just under three to The Railway in Docking (railwayinndocking.co.uk; 01485 518620), which is more of a local boozer.
Access A couple of the pitches have campervan access but the vast majority are car-free. Wheelbarrows are provided and you can occasionally blag a mini-tractor tow from the warden. The longest walk is no further than 150 yards from the car park.
Mobile phone signal This is a wild site for network coverage. O2 users will enjoy a few bars but, for most folks, Dreamy Hollow is nicely off the grid.
If it's full It's four miles to a popular family campsite beneath the sails of Bircham Windmill (birchamwindmill.co.uk; 01485 578393) or head out to the coast where there are a couple of year-round options (see p.66).

17

Fire & Stars

There are several ways to camp in this 47-acre stretch of woodland. You can pitch your tent in one of the 10 leafy clearings, each with a stone firepit and ample space to pin out your guy ropes, or you can go a little wilder and hang up a hammock instead. For the most intrepid, you can even build your own stick-and-moss shelter to sleep in, which has happened more than once and is a big hit with children (even if they do come crawling back to their parents' tent in the middle of the night).

Privately managed in partnership with the National Forest and Forestry England, Fire & Stars is open all year, bringing changing colours, not just through the seasons, but seemingly at different times of the day, as the sunlight breaks through the canopy at shifting angles. Money generated from campers goes into the upkeep of the wood, a heart-warming benefit of sleeping here. It's also pretty unsurprising, given there can't be much cost to running the facilities; there are portable toilets dotted here and there and the pub across the road has a small shower block that campers can use for a fee, but there's little else besides (including no mains water, so make sure you bring some bottles or a pre-filled tank with you).

Footpaths galore stripe the surrounding area, including the Ivanhoe Way and the National Forest Way, and it's five miles to English Heritage-owned Ashby De La Zouch Castle (english-heritage.org.uk; 01530 413343).

Nethercote Woods, Newton Burgoland, Leicestershire LE67 2SN
07961 765210 ● hello@fireandstars.co.uk ● fireandstars.co.uk

Open All year.
OS Explorer map 245 (SK 358 098).
Nearest pub It's a matter of yards to The Old Crown Inn (theoldcrownsnarestone.co.uk; 01530 270223), an 18th-century coaching inn with a restaurant, garden and play area.
Access There's parking in a grassy space by the campsite entrance, then walk in to pitches up to a maximum of 300 yards.
Mobile phone signal EE and Three give you access to the outside world, whereas Vodafone and O2 are more patchy.
If it's full There's a caravan park on the other side of the pub (newforestview.com; 07917 055169) but if you're looking for somewhere secluded, try the pitches at Purple Badger Camping (purplebadger.co.uk; 01162 595648).

18

Farm on the Hill

The clue is in the name at Farm on the Hill, five miles south of the Peak District. It's a farm, with camping pitches spread around 24 acres of meadows and young woods. And it's on a hill, with those who pitch at the very top of the site rewarded with sweeping views of the Churnet Valley and Weaver Hills. These raised spots are more exposed to the wind if the weather takes a turn, so ask for somewhere sheltered if the forecast isn't looking good, and its best to specify if you want the most secluded woodland pitches, since some are grouped together for more sociable camping.

In all, despite the off-grid facilities (composting loos and a solar-heated shower), this is very much a family site and it's a great place to introduce kids to basha building and campfire cooking for the first time. The farm is also home to Churnet Valley Cycle Hire, with a popular 10-mile-long riverside cycle route just down the lane, following the path of a former railway line.

For the wildest experience it's best to visit outside of the summer holidays, when you're likely to have the place almost entirely to yourselves. If you're worried that cloudy weather will scupper your solar shower then you needn't fear. A wood-fired stove, whose pipes run through a small sauna cabin, provides an alternative water-heating method. It takes around an hour for the shower to reach a comfortable temperature and you can relax in the sauna while you wait.

Manor House Farm, Prestwood, Uttoxeter, Staffordshire ST14 5DD ● 07597 841939 *farmonthehill.co.uk*

Open All year.

OS Explorer map 259 (SK 104 425).

Nearest pub It's a mile to the upmarket Duncombe Arms (duncombearms.co.uk; 01335 324275) with a spacious beer garden in summer.

Access Park at the farm then walk to the pitches. The 'Secret Garden' pitch does have parking alongside (just the other side of a hedge) and is best booked well in advance (there seem to be plenty of lazy bones who want it).

Mobile phone signal Reliable 4G on most networks.

If it's full It's three miles to Lower Micklin Touring Park (lmtp.co.uk; 07824 385138) for an altogether less wild experience, but try Rue Hill Campsite (ruehillcampsite.co.uk; 07932 472997; five and a half miles) for a more tent-friendly option.

19

The Campsite

Though it only opened in 2019, there's been a wild campsite of sorts on this 18-acre smallholding for years. Owners Caroline and Bobby previously opened up the space to friends, who would pitch their tents among the 3,000 native trees the couple have planted since they moved here a decade ago. Now the place is a bona fide campsite, though only for groups (of up to 30 people), who can hire the place out and enjoy the same freedoms as old chums.

Bobby is an avid wild camper and spent many a summer kayaking in Scotland, bivvying under the stars. He's also a carpenter, which comes in handy when you want to build an off-grid campsite – think log-cabin-esque composting toilet, a kitchen shelter under canvas sails and a log-fired shower in a tree. His quirky creations have accidentally created quite a comfortable place to camp but the proximity to nature, the secret pathways through the trees and the fact that you're the sole campers here ensures a suitably wild feel.

It's all of about 200 yards to the boundary of the Peak District National Park. You can walk from the campsite over Beeley Hill and down to the River Derwent, following it north to Chatsworth House, one of the most popular visitor attractions in the Peaks. The footpath falls upon numerous potential wild swimming spots too, particularly to the south of the famous country pile – perfect on a hot day.

Flash Lane, Darley Moor, Matlock, Derbyshire DE4 5LJ • **07985 310480**
thecampsite70@gmail.com • thecampsite.net

Open All year.
OS Explorer map OL24 (SK 292 659).
Nearest pub Nothing on the doorstep. It's three miles to the Grouse & Claret (grouseclaretpub.co.uk; 01629 733233) in Rowsely and the same to the Chatsworth Estate's Devonshire Arms (devonshirehotels.co.uk; 01629 733259).
Access Vehicle access to pitches is usually allowed but it depends on the weather and ground conditions.
Mobile phone signal It's wilderness for a lot of providers but O2 will reliably get you a few bars.
If it's full This is the Peak District, so there are plenty of options. Barn Farm (barnfarmcamping.com; 01629 650245) and Packhorse Farm (packhorsefarm.co.uk; 01629 580950) being the nearest spots for decent tent camping.

20

Piel Island

There are no cars, no showers and no electricity but there is a pub, a castle and a king. This 50-acre encampment, surrounded by the sea, is not a campsite at all; it's an island, a mini-territory that drifts in and out of the sea fret on foggy days. Visitors arrive by boat, checking in at The Ship Inn before scattering to spots of their choosing, tucked beside salty shrubbery for protection against the wind or in the shade of crumbling 14th-century turrets.

There was a time when camping here was free but popularity has put a premium on the luxury in recent years and the King (a title thought to date back 500 years and currently held by pub landlord Steve) now charges the princely sum of £5 to let you pitch by royal appointment. The money goes towards the upkeep of the isle, a Site of Special Scientific Interest, the protection of which also means that campfires are sadly not allowed. This rule extends to the sandy beach that wraps around the tear-drop-shaped territory and runs for miles when the tide recedes.

When the weather's clear, the views are spectacular. Behind nearby Barrow-in-Furness climbs the Lake District's forbidding Black Coombe mountain, shielding Whitfell and the Old Man of Coniston and, at night, the emptiness of the island overcomes Barrow's glow to reveal a vast array of stars. The isolation of the place is brought home on stormy days when the sea beats against the shore and the ferry stops running, making you glad you brought an extra tin of beans. Or glad the pub is still open.

Piel Island, Barrow-in-Furness, Cumbria LA13 0QN • 07516 453784
shipinn@pielisland.co.uk • pielisland.co.uk

Open All year (but the ferry is weather dependent).
OS Explorer map OL6 (SD 232 638).
Nearest pub The Ship Inn (pielisland.co.uk; 07516 453784) is the island's hub.
Access The Piel Island Ferry runs from Roa Island between 11am–5pm, weather permitting (£5 return for adults, £3 for children) then it's a two-minute walk from the slipway. It is also possible to walk across the sands at low tide from the south end of Walney Island (parking at Snab Point Car Park) but there's only a short window of around three to four hours, so be sure to consult the tide times.
Mobile phone signal Pretty reliable 4G on all networks.
If it's full It's an island. So the only local alternative is sleeping on a boat. Or pitching at a campsite on the mainland... how boring.

21

Turner Hall Farm

If you're looking for a truly remote Lake District campsite, you'd be hard pressed to find better than Turner Hall Farm in the national park's lesser-visited Duddon Valley. The reality is, it's not that far from civilisation, but it feels like the Middle of Nowhere, given the journey there.

The most spectacular way to arrive at Turner Hall Farm is to drive over the Wrynose Pass, a tortuous zigzag of steep road, often single-track and frequently hairpinned. If you're a nervous driver, take the safer long, winding road via Broughton Mills. Even from here, you have to get out of the car to open and close gates, an action loaded with the symbolism of leaving civilisation behind.

At the foot of the Old Man of Coniston, the campsite is best known among walkers and climbers, the attraction being its location rather than the facilities, but it's modernised just a little in recent years and proper showers and a washing-up area remove some of the almost-wild edge. On busy summer weekends, too, a population of fellow campers can take away from the isolated feel, but there's a raw, boulder-strewn beauty to the place, with private corners for sheltering in among the crags and drystone walls.

Weathered and worn, beaten and torn, Turner Hall merges into the rugged fell landscape and makes for the perfect place to practise getting off the grid before hiking up high for a night of wild camping proper.

Seathwaite, Broughton-in-Furness, Cumbria LA20 6EE • 01229 716420
turnerhallcampsite@gmail.com • duddonvalley.co.uk

Open Easter–November.
OS Explorer map OL6 (SD 232 962).
Nearest pub The Newfield Inn (newfieldinn.co.uk; 01229 716208), 10 minutes' walk down the road in the hamlet of Seathwaite, has real ale, a real fire, and real hearty food.
Access You can park beside your pitch.
Mobile phone signal This is total wilderness when it comes to coverage. You might as well leave your phone at home.
If it's full There are ample options in the Lake District; our pick of the more local bunch around Old Man of Coniston is Moss Side Farm (mosssidefarm.com; 07812 591151), a little further south.

*...there's a raw, boulder-strewn beauty to the place,
with private corners for sheltering in among the
crags and drystone walls.*

22

Gill Head Farm

Arrive at this Lakeland farm between Keswick and Penrith and you're met with plenty of campsite staples. There's a reception building, an open camping field and a clutch of modern glamping pods. So far, so standard. But ask to pitch in the secret riverside meadow and you're directed to a hidden, almost-wild camping spot found, incongruently, by driving through a tiny settlement of static caravans before crossing an old railway bridge and following a narrow, hedge-hugged track.

The secret meadow has space for just four or five pitches at the foot of a gentle slope, though it's not uncommon to have it all to yourself if you're there mid-week or outside of summer. The noise of the busy A66 is drowned out by the sound of Trout Beck, which babbles its way down a waterfall and along the edge of the meadow (the easiest place to refill your water if you don't fancy the trek back to the facilities block).

The long walk to the loo is the price to pay for such splendid isolation but it's well worth every footstep and an admitted sense of smugness arises from knowing you've chosen a spot that most campers on the site don't even know about. The only things that you lose by pitching in the hidden dell are the splendid views of mighty Blencathra afforded to the 'standard' camping meadow. You can hike the hulking mountain directly from the campsite or skip the first couple of low-level miles by driving down the road to the hamlet of Scales.

Troutbeck, Penrith, Cumbria CA11 0ST ● 01768 779953
enquiries@gillheadfarm.co.uk ● gillheadfarm.co.uk

Open Easter–November.
OS Explorer map OL4 (NY 380 268).
Nearest pub The Troutbeck Inn (thetroutbeckinn.co.uk; 017684 83635) is within 15 minutes' walking distance.
Access You can park on the track beside the riverside meadow, a matter of yards away, but not directly beside your tent.
Mobile phone signal Fine in the main camping meadow but in the dell of the secret riverside meadow you're generally out of signal.
If it's full If the hidden meadow is full try the main camping field. Otherwise head south towards Ulverston where The Quiet Site (thequietsite.co.uk; 01768 486337) offers a less wild setting but excellent eco credentials, good views and the nation's best campsite pub.

23

Hemscott Hill Farm

The campsite at Hemscott Hill Farm is rather elusive. Not only is it a 'pop-up' site, open for just a month or so each year but, on occasion, it doesn't open at all, thanks to a shifting focus on the farm towards hosting weddings and events instead. Recently, however, camping has staged a comeback and this popular pop-up has returned, a hidden sanctuary for coastal campers who like to pitch within earshot of the sea.

Campers can choose their pitch at the site, which is situated just off a quiet Northumberland coast road and across a field. There's a general meadow space but, for seclusion, smaller tents can be pitched right in among the dunes, hidden in a rolling sandscape that feels like a continuation of the choppy North Sea. On a windy day, a cacophony of crashing waves is the overwhelming soundtrack, along with sand scratching against your tent. But, whatever the weather, seven-mile-long Druridge Bay is a walker's delight and, when it's calm, flip-flopping through marram grass to the sea for a swim is a start to the day you won't forget.

Facilities are certainly wild. There is a freshwater tap and a composting loo, though even the latter was removed in 2020 so that just a chemical disposal point remained (details for 2021 onwards unconfirmed at the time of print) and there are no showers. Bring bikes to make the most of immediate access to Northumberland's Coast and Castles cycle route – magnificent Warkworth Castle (english-heritage.org.uk) is a 40-minute ride away.

Widdrington, Morpeth, Northumberland NE61 5EQ ● 01670 458118
hello@hemscotthill.com ● tractorsandtents.com

Open Mid July–mid August.
OS Explorer map 325 (NZ 281 951).
Nearest pub The Widdrington Inn (thewiddringtoninn.co.uk; 01670 760260) and The Plough Inn (theploughellington.co.uk; 07414 920292) in Ellington are the nearest at around two miles away.
Access The camping is 100 yards or so from a quiet coast road and you can park by your pitch (depending on how far into the dunes you stray).
Mobile phone signal Good for most. Patchy with Vodafone.
If it's full There are a couple of holiday parks around Creswell, just over a mile south of the farm. But for decent tent camping try Walkmill Campsite (walkmillcampsite.co.uk; 01665 710155) nine miles north near Warkworth.

On a windy day, a cacophony of crashing waves is the overwhelming soundtrack, along with sand scratching against your tent.

WALES

24

Into the Sticks

Much of this 22-acre smallholding on the banks of the Western Cleddau River is a designated Site of Special Scientific Interest, but more than half has been set aside for a few lucky campers, rarely numbering more than 25 people at any given time. There are just a handful of pitches, spread generously around a site that mixes woods, meadows and marshes and has particularly secluded spots for those with hammocks or bivvy bags.

Given the thoroughly wild feel of the place, facilities are surprisingly good. There are hot showers, toilets, a covered kitchen space and a barn that's been converted into a warm communal area with sofas and games. On rainy days impromptu wet-weather workshops are even organised, like bird-box building or arts and crafts using flotsam and driftwood. If you don't fancy getting involved, you can sidle off along the site's nature trail and take up watch beside the river. Otters have been spotted on brief forays here and you can sometimes find their spate left subtly along the bank.

It's a little over a mile to the nearest A road, whisking you north to Fishguard in around 15 minutes or south to Haverfordwest. And, though the campsite is inland and feels as off the beaten track as the name suggests, there's a treasure trove of beaches within a 20-minute drive, including Abercastle, Abereiddy and Newgale.

Letterston, Pembrokeshire SA62 5TF ● **01348 840968**
camp@intothesticks.co.uk ● *intothesticks.co.uk*

Open All year.
OS Explorer map OL35 (SM 930 291).
Nearest pub The Harp Inn (theharpatletterston.co.uk; 01348 840061) off the A40 a mile and a half away is technically the nearest pub but, for food, it's beaten hands down by Something's Cooking (somethingscooking.wales; 01348 840621) in Letterston, which has become one of the most renowned fish and chip shops in Pembrokeshire. It can be hard to get a table.
Access There's no parking at your pitch and the walk is a maximum of 250 yards.
Mobile phone signal You're in the sticks if you're with Three but other networks are surprisingly reliable.
If it's full Try the wildflower meadow camping at Preseli Glamping (preseliglamping. co.uk; 01348 837709), five miles away, and there are some relatively wild spots at Ty Parke Farm (typarke.co.uk; 01348 837384) seven miles away too.

…on the banks of the Western Cleddau River is a designated Site of Special Scientific Interest, but more than half has been set aside for a few lucky campers, rarely numbering more than 25 people at any given time.

25

Dragonfly Woodland Camping

It takes someone with a qualification in Renewable Energy and Engineering to create a campsite quite like this. "Wild camping with perks", is how graduate Jacob describes Dragonfly Wood. He's built picnic-bench shelters at each of the ten pitches, an eco-friendly shower block and the only power on the campsite is solar. Yet, despite the different structures around the place, the site, in general, is pleasantly low key and very well hidden among the trees.

The Bluebell pitch is the smallest and most tucked away, while other spots have been purposefully designed for groups of friends. All pitches come with log blocks and benches, sculpted out of the site's own birchwood and perfect for sitting around your campfire, and a couple of pitches have access for small campervans.

The owl-inhabited woodland is matched by the beauty of the wider surrounds. The campsite is set just back from the Daugleddau Estuary and it's not unusual for campers to arrive here with a kayak on the car roof.

Pretty Lawrenny village is a half-hour walk away and home to all the traditional staples – a shop, cricket club and 12th-century church. It's a little further to the quay, where a boat club is neighboured by a popular tearoom, which makes an ideal starting point for walks along the waterside footpath, taking you through the trees of National Trust-owned Cleddau Woodlands. The stretch around Benton Castle is a particularly quiet spot to stop for a swim at high tide (watch out for currents) and if you time it right you can even let the flow of the water carry you back to Lawrenny Quay.

Lawrenny, Kilgetty, Pembrokeshire SA68 0QD ● 07919 911611
jacob-dent@hotmail.co.uk ● dragonflycamping.co.uk

Open May–September.
OS Explorer map OL36 (SN 049 079).
Nearest pub You can walk less than a mile to the nearest pub, the Cresselly Arms (01646 651210) or drive 5 minutes to the Lawrenny Arms (01646 651367) or the Quayside Tearooms (quaysidelawrenny.co.uk; 01646 651574).
Access You can park at your pitch.
Mobile phone signal Better than nothing but don't expect 4G.
If it's full Try family-friendly Dewslake Farm (dewslakecamping.co.uk; 01646 672139) six miles south near Pembroke.

26

Cilrath Wood

Though it first opened in 2020, Cilrath Wood campsite feels like a place that time forgot. Over a mile from the nearest road, you arrive on a track with the Preseli Hills rising to greet you before a tunnel of hedgerows leads into the vale below. Here you're welcomed by an old hay meadow, an ancient woodland and a chocolate box 18th-century farmhouse. Time it right and you'll be greeted by farmers Pete and Jackie too, complete with a suitably vintage Land Rover to take your belongings to your pitch.

Campers can choose from five spots in the woods or five in the more open meadow but, wherever you pitch, there's plenty of space to roam. Brooks rise on the farm and tumble gently down to a small wildlife lake, while footpaths guide you on an amble through the wood. Arrive in spring and you'll get an undulating ocean of bluebells too.

Among it all there are two charming communal spaces – a silk parachute that hangs over a dell (an old 17th-century quarry) and a simple zinc-topped open barn where campers can socialise within view of the lake, catching the last of the evening light. Other facilities are rustic but surprisingly thorough given the site's size, including USB chargers, a fridge-freezer and fresh eggs, all in the shed by the campsite entrance.

Once back out on the road, Cilrath seems well connected. Pretty much every part of the Pembrokeshire Coast National Park is within a half-hour drive (the nearest beaches around Saundersfoot and Amroth are less than 20 minutes) and the local town of Narberth (two miles) was recently declared 'the happiest place to live in Wales'.

Cilrath Fach Farm, Narberth, Pembrokeshire SA67 7EY ● 01834 861106
camping@cilrath.co.uk ● cilrathwoodcamping.co.uk

Open Easter–October.
OS Explorer map OL36 (SN 113 169).
Nearest pub It's a four-minute drive or a half-hour walk into Narberth town, which has a wealth of pubs and cafés for its size. The Dragon Inn (marstons.co.uk; 018348 60257) is particularly popular while, for daytime bites, Spanish deli and café Ultracomida (ultracomida.co.uk; 01970 630686) is locally renowned.
Access There's limited vehicle access to a couple of the pitches, depending on the weather. Otherwise it's a walk of 50–150 yards from the parking area.
Mobile phone signal Good 3G across the site. 4G is a stretch, particularly in the trees.
If it's full Digs in the Wig (see p.102) and Dragonfly Woodland Camping (see p.96) are both within 10 miles.

Campers can choose from five spots
in the woods or five in the more
open meadow but, wherever you
pitch, there's plenty of space to roam.

27

Digs in the Wig

It's little known that, centuries ago, the Preseli Hills were once blanketed in miles upon miles of forest. Today the area is better known for its expanses of open lowland and beautifully bare hills but, in a 25-acre stretch of ancient wood, Digs in the Wig campsite boasts a spot in one of the few small patches of old forest that remain.

Home to just five pitches, there's fairly little to the site but, with a campfire pit, a composting loo and a little kitchen shelter at each, it certainly lends would-be wild campers a higher degree of comfort than first glances suggest. Along with the seclusion of each pitch, the campsite itself feels rather remote too. It's two miles to the nearest village, Maenclochog – where there's a newsagents, a café and a petrol station – so it's best to stock up on food before you arrive.

The surrounding Preselis have Special Area of Conservation status and are popular with walkers on the path of the prehistoric. From hillforts, like Foel Drygarn and Mynydd Carningli, to stone circles, like Gors Fawr, there are plenty of sights on your tent-step, while newer Llys y Fran Reservoir is two miles away and offers sailing, windsurfing and canoeing. Perhaps the most famous stretch of the Preselis is Cwm Gwaun (The Gwaun Valley), a bucolic basin of unfeasibly narrow lanes flanked by knuckle-bare mountains, just a 15-minute drive from the campsite. It's a walkers' paradise, made all the better by the characterful Dyffryn Arms pub (thedyffrynarms. com; 01639 636184) that awaits at the end of your trek.

Parc yr Eithin, New Moat, Clarbeston Road, Pembrokeshire SA63 4RJ ● 07747 166125
info@digsinthewig.co.uk ● digsinthewig.co.uk

Open Easter–October.
OS Explorer map OL35 (SN 051 248).
Nearest pub There's nothing within easy ambling distance but the nearest pub is also one of the most characterful: Tafarn Sinc (tafarnsinc.cymru; 01437 532214; four miles) looks like a tin shed but its interior, featuring wood-burners, sawdust-strewn floors and old photos from the area's mining days, make it an instant charmer.
Access If the weather's good you can get your car to most pitches.
Mobile phone signal There's a smidgen at the campsite (particularly for EE and Three users) but the Preselis are pretty patchy generally.
If it's full Into the Sticks (see p.92) and Cilrath Wood (see p.98) are both around 10 miles away, while it's five miles to Tir Bach Farm (tirbachfarm.co.uk; 01437 532362).

28

Nantgwynfaen Organic Farm

On the slopes of the Teifi Valley, Amanda and Ken Edward's smallholding is the centre point for a spread of diverse enterprises. Ken crafts Welsh oak and chestnut into bespoke furniture, while the hens scratching outside supply eggs to the organic farm shop. Their 175-year-old farmhouse, meanwhile, is also the quaint setting for a bed and breakfast with a couple of glamping options in the garden beyond.

The truly hidden spots at Nantgwynfaen Farm, however, are reserved for campers. Just five intimate pitches are scattered in disparate spots. They bear punny names like Hind Site and ConTented, while the best, Sun of a Pitch, is out of sight of all other campers, facing west over a dramatic steep valley that drops away to a hidden stream and offers a sublime canvas for sunsets.

If you're trying to camp wild you can cook over the campfire, watch for buzzards over the valley and enjoy bathing under a shower made from an old watering can. If you want more comforts, though, you can pay £15 to have breakfast in the farmhouse before spending a day out on the coast. It's 20 minutes to the nearest beach, yet, in summer, swimmers in the know head to the waterfall at Henllan instead, where deep pools are easily accessible just upstream of the arched stone bridge.

Nantgwynfaen, Penrhiwllan Road, Croeslan, Llandysul, Ceredigion SA44 4SR
01239 851914
amanda@organicfarmwales.co.uk ● *organicfarmwales.co.uk*

Open All year.
OS Explorer map 185 (SN 379 440).
Nearest pub A couple of miles down the road lies The Daffodil Inn (daffodilinn.co.uk; 01559 370343) at Penrhiwllan, a Michelin Guide-listed gastropub with a decent range of Welsh guest beers and stunning views across the valley from the dining room.
There's a good trail beside the stream below the campsite for the first half of the walk.
Access You can't park on your pitch but even the furthest is just 50 yards or so from the parking area.
Mobile phone signal Don't count your organically fed chickens. Signal is fairly non-existent at a lot of pitches but there's WiFi in the farmhouse if you really must.
If it's full There are a couple of tent pitches at riverside Henfryn Farm (henfrynfarm. co.uk; 01559 362840) but if they're taken try Firecrest Valley (firecrestvalley.co.uk; 07857 614744) a little further south.

...you can cook over the campfire, watch for buzzards over the valley and enjoy bathing under a shower made from an old watering can.

29

Pytingwyn Lane

There's been an informal campsite of sorts in this grassy dell, bordering the Brecon Beacons, for five or six years now but it's wild enough not to feature on any maps and is largely untraceable online. That explains why, much of the year, you can have the place almost to yourself, particularly if you pitch in the light woodland, which covers around half of the four-acre space.

The River Honddu forms the boundary along one edge – it's great for splashing but, in summer, only deep enough in a handful of places to swim – and you can try fishing for trout, if you've brought your tackle. George the horse nibbles at the other side of the campsite, always of interest to young children.

Things remain pretty much unchanged here since the day the place first opened. Don't expect showers or electricity and, if you're not alone, you might have to wait to use the one composting loo provided – with only five or six pitches at any one time, it won't take long.

Though the highest mountain in the Brecon Beacons is less than 10 miles from your doorstep, one of the best walks is an easy five-mile circular loop straight from the campsite. Follow the lane and a bridleway up to the top of Pen-y-crug, an Iron-Age hill fort overlooking the Usk Valley with striking views of Pen-y-fan to the south and the Black Mountains away to the east. Then tumble down into the charming town of Brecon, busy with fellow walkers and outdoorsy types, and back along the riverside footpath to your tent.

Pytingwyn Lane, Brecon, Powys LD3 9LN ● 07983 722547
davidjmorris2@outlook.com

Open Easter–September.
OS Explorer map OL12 (SO 039 311).
Nearest pub Brecon has the closest pubs and everything else you need. Brecon Tap (01874 622353) is the place for real ales and a cosy atmosphere (and tasty pies), while The Hours Café and Bookshop (thehoursbrecon.co.uk; 01874 622800) is a rainy-day joy.
Access Park beside your pitch (or beside the wood if you're camping in the trees).
Mobile phone signal Bizarrely good coverage, with 4G for all.
If it's full It's less than two miles to another excellent, small, riverside campsite at Priory Mill Farm (priorymillfarm.co.uk). However, they don't accept children under the age of 13. For more options, see p.110.

30

Middle Ninfa Farm

Steep hillsides aren't usually conducive to camping but various scoops and hollows on the slopes of Middle Ninfa Farm make it not just a pleasant place to pitch but also an excellent neighbour-free amphitheatre for looking out across the Vale of Usk in the Brecon Beacons.

There are eight secluded pitches in total, plus three or four in the 'main' camping area nearest the rudimentary facilities block that comprises two compost loos, a cold shower and a filtered water tap. 'Stone Circle' is the farthest flung pitch; it occupies a natural terrace behind an ancient stone wall that's long since collapsed, while 'Deri' ('Oak' in Welsh) sits beneath a copse of giant oak and beech trees. The former is ideal for hammock camping, while the latter has one of the best views over the farm, facing north towards the horn-shaped Skirrid Mountain.

Though all of the pitches are suitably wild and isolated, campers who don't like company should pick a spot in the woods. If not, you may wake to Fly the horse nibbling the grass around your guy lines. She likes campfires and befriending campers but is generally careful not to step on anything she shouldn't.

A short but steep trek upwards leads to the Woodland Trust's scenic Punchbowl nature reserve, complete with lake and woods, while a tumble two miles down leads you to Abergavenny town, which has all the essential amenities.

Llanellen near Abergavenny, Monmouthshire NP7 9LE ● 01873 854662
bookings@middleninfa.co.uk ● middleninfa.co.uk

Open All year.
OS Explorer map OL13 (SO 285 116).
Nearest pub A map on the campsite shows the footpath route to the award-winning Goose and Cuckoo (thegooseandcuckoo.co.uk; 01873 880277), three miles away in Upper Llanover. Alternatively, there are plenty of options in Abergavenny.
Access You can't park at your pitch. If you choose the 'main' site you'll still be near your boot, otherwise it's a walk of 70–170 yards depending on the spot you choose.
Mobile phone signal Reliable 4G beaming from Abergavenny.
If it's full Pyscodlyn Farm Caravan & Camping Site (pyscodlyncaravanpark.com; 01873 853271) and Park Farm (parkfarm-campsite.co.uk; 01873 812183) are four miles and eight miles respectively, but the off-grid campsite beside ruined Llanthony Priory (llanthonycamping.co.uk; 01873 890359; 15 miles) is the best nearby pick for tenters.

31

Gorfanc

While visitors flock to Snowdonia National Park further north, the open spaces like Trannon Moor, nestled in a fold of the Cambrian Mountains, remain blissfully untouched but for the ubiquitous grazing sheep and the steady turn of distant wind turbines. Tethered to the little village of Carno by a narrow, mile-and-a-half-long road, the 11-acre smallholding of Gorfanc edges the empty space and has a rustic way of life about it to match.

Owners Pippa and Rob live in a stone-built cottage on the site, which is also home to a tiny two-person rental called The Hideaway. In the nooks and scoops of the land beyond there are six wild camping pitches, some hugged by shaggy fern-covered slopes, others beside a stream. Drinking water and a flushing toilet are available to use back at the house and you can pay £1 to have a shower. Or save up your change to buy logs for the campfire or fresh eggs and honey (don't be surprised to find the hens pecking around your pitch each day).

It's possible to walk for miles here with only sheep paths to follow and not another soul in sight. When the weather's hot, the stream is great for splashing about (and a rinse off if you haven't used the shower) but, for a proper swim, you can thread your way back east to the River Severn or climb to the three lakes above the village of Clatter – Llyn Mawr is a nature reserve and Llyn Du is for fishing but, if you're discrete, Llyn n Tawr is good for a bracing dip.

The Gorfanc Hideaway, Carno, Caersws, Powys SY17 5JP ● 01686 420423
downthetrack@the-gorfanc-hideaway.co.uk ● the-gorfanc-hideaway.co.uk

Open All year.
OS Explorer map 215 (SN 948 956).
Nearest pub It's a mile and a half to Carno, where there are two pubs, The Aleppo (thealeppo.co.uk; 01686 420210) and Tybrith (01686 420206).
Access No parking at your pitch, but there are spaces up by the cottage, and the walk is around 100 yards.
Mobile phone signal Excellent.
If it's full It's 10 miles to Gwalia Farm (see p.114) and not-so-wild Cringoed Caravan Park (cringoedcaravanpark.wales; 01650 521237) is en route, at seven miles.

32

Gwalia Farm

Since arriving at this partially wooded and watery smallholding in 1979, the owners of Gwalia Farm have learnt to be self-sufficient. Chickens scratch in the front yard, there's a small flock of sheep and a beautiful Jersey cow called Daisy, and surplus veg from the gardens are stoically pickled or stored away in jars. The same resourcefulness is largely expected of campers, who arrive here, in the hills edging the Dyfi Valley, and are largely left to their own devices to explore the Eden-like space beyond the farmhouse.

Surrounded by trees, Gwalia is a blessing for anyone with strong hunterer-gatherer DNA. Campfires are permitted, stray pieces of wood can be picked up and used and the owners sell bundles. There's usually only a handful of campers present at any one time and they are spread far enough apart so that all you'll see of your neighbours are wafts of campfire smoke rising from the other side of the rushes. Don't expect a queue for the showers, either. There aren't any. Though you can pay to use one in the farmhouse if you're in particular need.

A couple of ponds add to the serenity of the place and attract an abundance of dragon and damsel flies, frogs, newts and toads. Campers can swim in the top pond if they feel like joining the amphibians, or drive the five minutes to Cemmaes, where there are some good spots for swimming in the Dyfi on hot summer days. Well placed for walkers, too, the farm is directly beside Glyndŵr's Way, a 135-mile National Trail taking in the moorland and hills south of Snowdonia, including Moel Eiddew, which rises invitingly beside the farm.

Cemmaes, Machynlleth, Powys SY20 9PZ ● 01650 511377
amy@gwaliafarm.co.uk ● gwaliafarm.co.uk

Open All year.
OS Explorer map 215 (SH 854 047).
Nearest pub At the bottom of the hill, the Penrhos Arms (penrhosarms.com; 01650 511243) is a gorgeous stone hotel that serves above-average pub grub.
Access No vehicle access to the pitches but it's only a short walk – the closest pitch is about 15 yards from the parking area.
Mobile phone signal Suprisingly decent on all networks.
If it's full It's not far to similarly small Gorfanc (see p.112) or Smugglers Cove Boatyard (see p.116) but Gwerniago Farm (gwerniago.co.uk; 01654 791227), at the foot of Cader Idris has long been a firm Cool Camping family favourite.

33

Smugglers Cove Boatyard

A former slate works and quay, Smugglers Cove has continued its existence as a small working boatyard with a commanding location beside the Dyfi Estuary in Snowdonia. Look past this unassuming nautical disguise, however, and the place is also home to a tiny handful of camping pitches, secreted away along the waterside footpath and piggybacking off the boatyard's old toilet and shower facilities.

Bag one of the four exclusive spots and you're in for a treat. Beyond your tent flaps is a scene that changes as much within the hour as most campsites enjoy across a season. Brew your morning coffee over a fire as high tide laps your toes and sailing boats to and fro across the estuary. Come lunchtime, it's become a private beach, the water withdrawing to a narrow sliver in the sand where lapwings, redshanks and long-legged birds totter along its edges.

The RSPB Ynys-hir Nature Reserve is on the opposite shore, so it's no surprise the wildlife here is so prevalent and the presence of a nearby A-road does little to disturb the birds or the camping experience, thanks to a decent screening of trees. When the tide is out, you can walk the three miles to the artsy harbour town of Aberdyfi, or hunt for crabs in leftover pools of water. Beside the yard there's also an old fishing boat that now identifies as a permanent landlubbing cabin. With a piano, a kitchen, and a wood-burning stove on board it makes for an excellent communal space if it's not already booked out for private use.

Frongoch, Aberdyfi, Gwynedd LL35 0RG ● 01654 767037
smugglerscoveboatyard@gmail.com ● smugglerscove.info

Open Easter–November.
OS Explorer map OL23 (SN 66 2972).
Nearest pub There's nothing particularly on your doorstep. Drive the five minutes into Aberdyfi, where The Penhelig Arms (sabrain.com; 01654 767215) is the closest spot to the campsite.
Access From the signed parking area just off the A493, walk under the railway to the estuaryside where you'll find the boatyard, then follow the footpath round to the individual pitches. The furthest is around 250 yards from your car.
Mobile phone signal Reliable for most; O2 and Vodafone have the biggest black spots.
If it's full Head inland to Gwerniago Campsite (gwerniago.co.uk; 01654 791227) or Gwalia Farm (see p.114).

34

Graig Wen

It's a tale of two campsites at Graig Wen. The 'conventional' touring site is home to hardstandings, a couple of tent pitches, yurts, a shepherd's hut and B&B rooms in a characterful old slate-cutting mill. Follow a steep track through the oaks, however, and you're led out to a 40-acre patchwork of meadows beside the Mawddach Estuary, where just 18 car-free pitches are scattered.

How wild you want to be is up to you. The meadows are stitched together by drystone walls and flanks of trees, so you can choose from the family-friendly paddock nearest the parking or trek through gates and up slopes to the most secluded pitches, like Monk's Corner or Buzzards Perch, set atop a high bluff with a stream babbling below.

Footpaths also lead down to the Mawddach Trail, a popular cycle route following a former branch of the Great Western Railway. Follow it six miles east to the shops of Dolgellau or three miles west to Barmouth and the beach, taking in the long wood-slat bridge that crosses the yawning mouth of the estuary. From here you can look back and admire the campsite's backdrop: 2,930-foot Cadair Idris to the rear, a grand mountain fortress and the most well-known peak in southern Snowdonia, with the smaller lump of Cefn Hir Hill Fort below, just a short scramble away from your tent.

Arthog, Near Dolgellau, Gwynedd LL39 1YP • 01341 250482
hello@graigwen.co.uk • graigwen.co.uk

Open All year (but the lower camping meadows from May–mid September only).
OS Explorer map OL23 (SH 654 157).
Nearest pub Good pub grub can be found at The George III Hotel (georgethethird.pub; 01341 422525) which is five minutes' drive or an hour and a half's delightful walk along the estuary cycle trail.
Access You can park beside your pitch in the top, year-round touring site but not in the lower estuary meadows. In the lower meadows the walk ranges from 50 yards up to 750 yards if you want to find the most secluded pitches.
Mobile phone signal It depends on where you are across the 45-acre site. Good signal for most, except O2. Choose the Sycamore pitch or Ash Corner if you want to banish your inbox for good.
If it's full Hafod Dywyll Campsite (hafoddywyllcampsite.co.uk; 01341 423444), three miles east of Graig Wen, is an excellent, informal campsite, well placed for climbing Cader Idris.

Footpaths lead down to the Mawddach Trail,
a popular cycle route following a former branch
of the Great Western Railway. Follow it three
miles west to Barmouth and the beach, taking
in the long wood-slat bridge that crosses the
yawning mouth of the estuary.

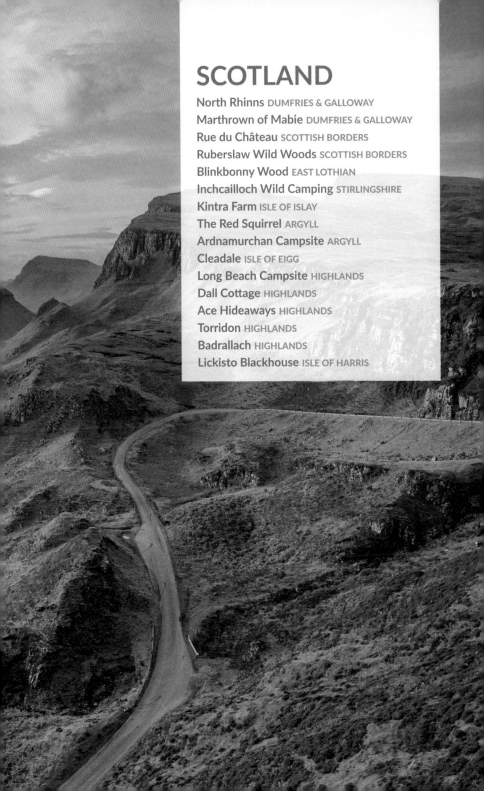

SCOTLAND

35

North Rhinns

Off a tiny backroad on the Rhins of Galloway, the hammerhead-shaped peninsula on Scotland's southwestern edge, this tiny campsite feels more like a semi-wild garden. And, in a way, it is. When the Googes first moved here just over a decade ago they found a small forest beyond their white-stone cottage, run wild with bracken and brambles, and saw the potential to create the sort of campsite they had always wanted to stay at themselves. Inch by inch, they hand-cut pitches according to the shape of the land and the feel of the space so each spot has its own character – one is perfect for watching the sunset, another completely lost amid the trees or favoured by grazing deer at dawn. Find the one that suits you best and settle down.

The longer you stay here, the more you discover about this deceptive site. The trees you thought were all pines also include young oaks and odd exotics (is that really a eucalyptus?). That odd 'ack-ack' noise isn't a misfiring tractor but a boisterous buzzard. And, yes, the road really is that quiet.

The place is well managed and there are a couple of hardstanding pitches near the washblock so, all in all, it's on the milder side of wild but the site's tiny size and the fact that, outside of weekends, you almost always have the place to yourself, gives it a remote feel. There's not much to do besides wildlife watching, combing empty beaches and striking out along the dramatic coastal path. Drive the 15–20 minutes over endless cattle grids to Killantringan Lighthouse for an excellent starting point then hike the hour south to the colourful harbour town of Portpatrick.

Glengyre Cottage, Leswalt, Stranraer, Wigtownshire, Dumfries & Galloway DG9 0RG
01776 853630 ● enquiries@northrhinnscamping.co.uk ● northrhinnscamping.co.uk

Open Easter–October (and potentially outside of this by arrangement).
OS Explorer map 309 (NW 994 651).
Nearest pub There's nothing within a five mile radius. Head back to Stranraer for a takeaway or drive eight miles to Portpatrick, where there's a trio of waterfront pubs.
Access There are three campervan pitches and two tent pitches you can park beside, while the pitches among the trees are little more than 50 yards from a parking space.
Mobile phone signal Don't count on it. Think of the place as a silent retreat.
If it's full There are plenty of caravan parks on the peninsula but nothing else for decent tent camping. It's a 35-minute drive back east to characterful Balloch O'Dee (01671 830708; ballochodee.com), where you can camp alongside free-roaming ponies.

36

Marthrown of Mabie

The final mile to Marthrown of Mabie, just south of Dumfries, is a gravelly track (made all the more disconcerting by an 'authorised vehicles only' sign at the entrance) that seems to go on for twice that distance and gradually climbs into the trees. The land here is looked after by Forestry Scotland (hence the signs) and the campsite, sat atop a false brow of the hill, is at the whims of their forestry work.

When we first visited a few years ago it was a woodland campsite, with space to pitch tents among gangly pines. More recently, great swathes of the hilltop have had a haircut, so that the campsite now occupies a less wooded but no less wild space, with piles of timber forming walls and nooks, young saplings growing afresh and tree stumps offering endless makeshift tables and places to perch. The lopping of trees has also revealed a staggering view, looking south over the Solway Firth and to the distant Lake District fells beyond.

Anyone who wants a wilder camping experience will feel at home here and, as always, the further you walk from the communal kitchen, dining room and shower block (set around a courtyard), the quieter the spot you're likely to find. It's mountain bikers, however, who are the real regulars. Along with marked walking trails, Mabie Forest is one of the world-class 7stanes mountain biking centres that span the south of Scotland and caters for beginners through to the most expert riders. There's no bike hire shop, so you'll need to bring your own, but it's well worth it and it makes for an exhilarating way to earn your pint at the hotel at the bottom of the hill.

Mabie Forest, Near Dumfries, Dumfries & Galloway DG2 8HB • 01387 247900
info@marthrownofmabie.co.uk • marthrownofmabie.com

Open All year.
OS Explorer map 313 (NX 941 717).
Nearest pub Back at the bottom of the forestry road the swanky looking Mabie House Hotel (mabiehousehotel.co.uk; 01387 263188) has a cosy and more informal bar alongside the restaurant and caters well to mountain bikers.
Access Parking is beside the forestry track, then it's a 200-yard walk to the camping area.
Mobile phone signal Not bad but don't plan to rely on 4G to find the place (and it's well worth downloading some directions beforehand as it can be tricky).
If it's full It's not far as the crow flies, but a half-hour drive, to Caerlaverock Castle Corner Campsite (01387 216215), a small, basic site popular with tourers within walking distance of 13th-century Caerlaverock Castle.

37

Rue du Château

There's no château at Rue du Château. And the landscape – sheep-nibbled upland, rugs of pine trees and barren hills like Wolfelee, Bonchester and Rubers Law – is notably Scottish in appearance. So why the name? It seems it was destiny. And a mystery. A battered old French road sign has been part of the tree at the farm's entrance since the current owners moved here. And, for the campsite at least, the name has stuck.

There is something a bit French about the camping experience though. For starters it's exceptionally laid back. There are mown spaces along the banks of Harwood Burn but with a further 40 acres of rough grassland at your disposal you're invited to go for a wander and simply pitch where you please. When the sun is out the river makes an inviting place to paddle, swim or drift on an inflatable, imagining, perhaps, you're on a tiny tributary of the River Dordogne or Loire. Facilities are also modelled on a famous French trend: Minimalism. There are no showers, no electricity and a horse trailer houses the porta-toilet.

The wildest places to pitch are among trees further upstream, where wild primroses grow, or up near the tear-shaped pond where resident ducks tend to relax before marching back down to the Burn. The farm is also home to an inquisitive gypsy cob and a miniature Shetland pony called Teesh. There's ample wildlife too – red squirrels, deer, and badgers – and, though midges aren't much of a problem, it's worth bringing repellent for the horseflies – remember: Scotland, not France.

Bonchester Bridge, Hawick, Scottish Borders TD9 9RZ ● 07581 503340
rue-du-chateau.weebly.com

Open 28 days per year; check online for details.
OS Explorer map 331 (NT 584 096).
Nearest pub It's just under two miles to the recently well-renovated Horse & Hounds (horseandhoundbonchesterbridge.com; 01450 860645), a coaching inn dating back to 1701 with a garden that extends down to the riverside.
Access Park on the gravel at the bottom of the drive. The campsite reception is the house in the courtyard, not the main farmhouse. Then access is through the small red gate opposite, walk left across the field to find your pitch. Anything from 50–500 yards.
Mobile phone signal As rare as rocking horse manure.
If it's full It's not far to Ruberslaw Wild Woods (see p.130) or cross into Northumberland and try less-wild Kielder Campsite (kieldercampsite.co.uk; 01434 239257; 15 miles).

38

Ruberslaw Wild Woods

Ruberslaw Wild Woods is rightfully renowned among the camping fraternity. The site's main setting, within an Edwardian walled garden, complete with an old glass house, an ornamental pond and a croquet lawn, is a thing of real beauty and creates a sheltered, sociable enclave for families. For wild campers, however, the real treat lies beyond.

With 500 acres of upland at their disposal, the Bailey family haven't stopped at the garden. Instead, a handful of composting loos and freshwater taps have been scattered in select, wooded spots around the farm, some almost half a mile from the main camping hub. Groups can book pitches at 'Castle View', set in a conifer copse with views of an old tower across the Teviot Valley, while individual campers can trek the 20 minutes to 'Geldswing Lookout' and pitch in woods sheltered by a stone dyke. The latter spot also enjoys the best view of the hill that inspired the campsite's name.

Conical Rubers Law is, in fact, a volcano, and owes its shape to an eruption some 330 million years ago. It's a puff-inducing climb from the campsite and has faint remains of both an Iron-Age hill fort and a Roman signal station around the summit. From here you can look down on Hawick, Bonchester Bridge (see p.128) and the local village of Denholm, where poet Dr John Leyden was born, later penning poems about the hill.

Spital Tower, Denholm, Hawick, Scottish Borders TD9 8TB ● 01450 870092
reception@ruberslaw.co.uk ● ruberslaw.co.uk

Open March–October.
OS Explorer map 331 (NT 586 178).
Nearest pub The neighbouring village of Denholm, 20–25 minutes' scenic walk over the hill (or five minutes' drive for those in a particular hurry), has two good pubs: The small, almost coffee-house-like Fox and Hounds Inn (01450 870247) and the more spacious, low-ceilinged Auld Cross Keys (crosskeysdenholm.co.uk; 01450 870305).
Access There's parking near the entrance to the walled garden, so campers in the main area needn't walk far. Wild campers booking the wooded group pitches, however, have a 15–20-minute walk on their hands, depending on the spot they choose, while the wildest individual pitches are slightly further.
Mobile phone signal Not bad given the quiet location, best with Three and EE.
If it's full Not much locally by way of good tent camping alternatives. There's usually plenty of space at the camping and caravan club site just north of Jedburgh though (campingandcaravanningclub.co.uk; 01835 863393).

39

Blinkbonny Wood

The Wray family has owned Blinkboony Wood in East Lothian since 2002 and has welcomed small tents here for over a decade. Even so, camping remains little more than a sideline. This 100 acres of mixed pine and broadleaf on the edge of the Lammermuir Hills has only a handful of small clearings for tents. (It's difficult to tell how many there are, since the wood is so vast and the number of campers so few that you're unlikely to encounter anyone.) And it's all so far from any road that you'd need a high-powered Spooks-style surveillance kit to detect any sound.

Just around the hill from the pitches sits a log cabin offering a snug vantage-point for spotting birdlife and deer. And if you look back towards Edinburgh, you can see the rump of Arthur's Seat rising into the sky. The views from the pitches are none too shabby, either. They're a bit subtler, though, looking out over the soft farmland towards the sea, with the bird-splattered Bass Rock poking out of the water, and Traprain Law in the distance.

Facilities are nothing more than a composting loo. No showers, no running water and no electricity, though you can buy firewood from the back of an old horsebox and log benches and firepits are provided at each pitch. Bring bikes if you fancy the three-mile ride to the pretty village of Gifford or set out on foot to explore the surrounding hills, clad in a purple carpet of heather in later summer and autumn.

Long Yester, Near Gifford, East Lothian EH41 4PL ● 01620 825034
blinkbonny99@gmail.com

Open March–September.
OS Explorer map 351 (NT 541 642).
Nearest pub The weirdly named Goblin Ha in Gifford (goblinha.com; 01620 810244) is a typical small village pub and hotel. Don't go for the bistro; head for the small cosy bar at the side of the hotel.
Access Cars aren't allowed in the wood. There's a parking area at the main gate then it's a 5–10-minute walk to your pitch.
Mobile phone signal Imagine going into a deep cave and then finding another cave within that cave.
If it's full It's 30 minutes to the rather tame camping and caravanning club site at Lauder (campingandcaravanningclub.co.uk; 02476 475426) or 50 minutes south to the tent-only campsite Shepherd's Rest (shepherds-rest.co.uk; 07548 203430).

40

Inchcailloch Wild Camping

Who doesn't dream of camping on a tiny island? Near the eastern shore of Loch Lomond, this 130-acre isle is a designated National Nature Reserve and a sanctuary for birds and plant life. The only access is by boat, either by paddling a canoe and beaching in the soft sandy cove of Port Bawn or by taking the short ferry from Balmaha then trekking the half-mile path across the rump of the island's back. The campsite itself is rudimentary. There are compost loos but no showers, running water or refuse collection, so you'll need to fill up water containers in the boatyard before you disembark and pack out rubbish with you. And though fires are allowed, foraging for wood is a definite no no.

Bagging a pitch here isn't without its trials. Given the sensitive nature of Inchcailloch and its habitats, there's a maximum of 12 campers at any one time (and group sizes are limited to six people) and you can't stay longer than two nights. Pair that with the short and strict pre-booking process and it presents you with Charlie and the Chocolate Factory chances of getting to visit (see below for other options). Snag the golden ticket when the site first opens in spring, however, and you can enjoy swathes of bluebells and wild garlic, while wood warblers make their nests here in April and May. A warden visits daily to check permits and can help answer questions you may have about the wildlife or the surrounding landmarks. Where did the remains of the medieval church come from? Which peak is Ben Lomond, Bein Bhreac or Beinn Dubh? And what are the odds of getting to pitch here again this century?

Inchcailloch, Balmaha, Drymen, Stirlingshire G63 0JQ ● 01389 722600
inchcailloch@lochlomond-trossachs.org ● lochlomond-trossachs.org

Open March–September.
OS Explorer map OL39 (NS 407 900).
Nearest pub Does the phrase 'uninhabited island' mean nothing to you?
Access Access is by boat, kayak or canoe (anchor in the bay or beach your vessel) or by ferry from Balmaha (balmahaboatyard.co.uk; 01360 870214). A path leads off the jetty; after 100 yards you'll come to signs and a map with directions to the campsite (about 20 minutes' walk). A waterbus also runs from Balloch and Luss (lochlomond-trossachs.org).
Mobile phone signal As absent as you'd expect on an tiny off-grid island.
If it's full The national park has a number of similarly basic, semi-formal sites. Visit Loch Chon or Loch Achray (lochlomond-trossachs.org) or Sallochy Campsite (forestryandland. gov.scot; 01360 870142) or buy a permit and try the park's low-cost wild camping areas.

41

Kintra Farm

Just a short ferry hop from the Mull of Kintyre, Islay is relatively accessible without a full expedition party and a six-week supply of Kendal Mint Cake, but it still has the remote feel befitting of an island. There's not much here apart from birdlife and whisky distilleries and the isle has a good claim to being Scotland's whisky capital, boasting many of the finest, darkest, peatiest malts around from the south of the island as well as some less pungent spring-water malts from the north.

The site at Kintra is a working farm that just happens to have great beach frontage fringed with grassy dunes – a Site of Special Scientific Interest for chough and Arctic tern. You can shelter down in one of the dips or pitch the tent (make it a strong, three-season one) up high if you want that real wind-in-your-hair, salt-on-the-skin feel. The bonus for the brave is the view of the stretching sands of the Traigh Mhòr sweeping off to the north with the bare hills behind and the Rhinns of Islay across the choppy waters of Laggan Bay.

Facilities include hot showers and access to laundry facilities and you can park beside your pitch. So, in all, Kintra is on the more convenient side of 'wild'. But, outside of the summer peak, you're liable to have the place almost entirely to yourself.

Out on the water are all kinds of possibilities for bodyboard and sail, surfboard and kite. Or you could just enjoy a swim. Whatever you do, it's only a short scramble back into the marram grass and your tent for a warming dram of one of the local tipples.

Port Ellen, Isle of Islay PA42 7AT ● 01496 302051
bookings@kintrafarm-islay.co.uk ● kintrafarm-islay.co.uk

Open April–September.
OS Explorer map 352 (NR 320 484).
Nearest pub It's a 10-minute drive back to Port Ellen, where there's the White Hart (01496 300120) and The Ardview Inn (01496 302014).
Access You can park beside your pitch.
Mobile phone signal Three and EE generally tease you with some coverage here and there but don't expect much.
If it's full There's a site at the Port Mòr Centre, just south of Prince Charlotte, a 35-minute drive away (01496 850441).

42

The Red Squirrel

Thanks to its recent cinematic exploits, most notably in the James Bond film *Skyfall*, Glencoe is now one of Scotland's most world-renowned locations. But the tourist hype is worth it and it doesn't take much hiking to get away from the buses and busy laybys along the A82. From the moment you descent off the barren wastelands of Rannoch Moor, it's clear you're approaching somewhere special, as the road dips to acknowledge huge glacial massifs on either flank and the bulging knuckles of the Three Sisters. Turn off before the foot of the glen, down a narrow road that takes you past the legendary Clachaig Inn and, eventually, you'll find The Red Squirrel.

Spread across 20 acres of meadow and woodland with a couple of burns snaking through it, The Red Squirrel describes itself as a 'casual farm site' with no official pitches. In reality, like the glen, it's become rather well known in recent years, but push through to the end of the camp and follow the overgrown trail (you'll think you have gone the wrong way) and you can still find some wilder spots, tucked on an isolated island with great views. Elsewhere, a freshwater pool invites any camper brave enough to take the plunge and, in most spaces, you're allowed to have a campfire up until 11pm (handy for keeping the midges at bay).

Walkers are most at home here. Try the raised valley of Coire Gabhail ('the lost valley') or the short but steep hike from the campsite up to the Pap of Glen Coe, the perfect place to look out on Ballachulish and Loch Leven. Any hard day ends in the Clachaig Inn at the top of the road, where the Boots Bar has hundreds of malt whiskies. And from there it's an easy downhill stumble back to the tent.

Glencoe, Argyll PH49 4HX ● 01855 811256
office@redsquirrelcampsite.co.uk ● redsquirrelcampsite.co.uk

Open All year (closed over the Christmas and New Year period).
OS Explorer map 384 (NN 120 573).
Nearest pub Walk three quarters of a mile up the road to the Clachaig Inn (clachaig.com; 01855 811252); the restaurant is good but the Boots Bar has more atmosphere.
Access You can drive to most pitches but, for the wilder spots beside the River Coe, you'll have to walk 50 yards or so.
Mobile phone signal Not as bad if you're with Three but a black hole for most.
If it's full There's a Camping and Caravanning Club site 10 minutes away but we'd pick lochside Caolasnacon (kinlochlevencaravans.com; 01855 831279; five and half miles).

43

Ardnamurchan Campsite

Ancient Celtic traditions say that over the western sea, beyond the edge of any map, lies the afterlife. Sitting at Ardnamurchan campsite it's certainly easy to believe, as you watch the sun torch the ocean between the scattered Hebrides, that you're as close as you can get to Heaven on Earth.

The site clings to the coast just a few miles from the tip of a rocky finger that's as far west as Britain goes. You approach it (slowly) via a ferry and a sinuous single-track road that hems in the crumpled and craggy landscape and makes getting here an escapade in itself.

At first glance, the campsite certainly appears rough-and-ready – a slice of wild hillside only just tamed – but as you settle in you'll appreciate how every pitch has been cut from the slope and levelled, to provide sea views down the Sound of Mull to Morven and Mull, as well as a flat spot to pitch. The wildest spaces are down by the shore, where you'll be lulled to sleep by the wash of wave on rock.

Facilities are basic and quaintly ramshackle and the place lacks that real wild camping feel of being cut off from other campers – the site is only small – but with such a remote location it can never be described as busy. Should you feel the need to escape, the foreshore is rough, rocky and just right for a scramble, while some of the loveliest and emptiest beaches on the planet can be found nearby.

Ormsaigbeg, Kilchoan, Acharacle, Argyll PH36 4LL ● **01972 510766**
stay@ardnamurchancampsite.com ● *ardnamurchancampsite.com*

Open April–September.
OS Explorer map 390 (NM 470 629).
Nearest pub The recent closure of the Sonachan Hotel on the way to Ardnamurchan lighthouse is a blow but there's a fun coffee shop in an old stable at the lighthouse that's worth a visit. Bar meals and finer dining are on offer at the Kilchoan House Hotel (kilchoanhotel.co.uk; 01972 510200), a mile and a half away.
Access You can park by most pitches.
Mobile phone signal Signal seems to come and go with the waves. Don't count on it.
If it's full Lochan nan al Campsite (ardnamurchancamping.co.uk; 07435 624280) is just up the road, but caters more to campervans and caravans than tent campers. The next good spot is Resipole Farm (resipole.co.uk; 019674 31235) on the north shore of Loch Sunart, about 50 minutes' drive.

44

Cleadale

Nothing can prepare you for the view at Cleadale but the ferry certainly tries. Dolphins are a common sight and the Isle of Eigg itself gets evermore spectacular as you approach, with its serried banks of sheer cliffs and the insolent snub nose of An Sgurr towering over the harbour. Any geologists on your boat will be in heaven; birdwatchers may well be spontaneously combusting. But it's only when the local minibus rattles its way up and over the ludicrous ribbon of tarmac that passes for a road and drops you down into the cluster of crofts in the island's northern corner that you really get it.

First you look seawards – a sweep of green land, a white sand beach, a shining Hebridean sound and the jagged crown of the cuillin of Rum across the water. Then you heft your bag and turn to look at the campsite – and realise you will be staying at the bottom of a vast and curving cliff, an amphitheatre tiered infinitely steeply as if for the sole purpose of giving the eagles a braw place from which to observe the sunset.

The campsite itself is as wild and wonderful as its setting. The pitches aren't the flattest, there are two composting loos and water comes from a well. But you can pay £2 to use the shower in the owners' house if you get muddy while out exploring. There are two white sand beaches within a 15-minute walk; one, the Singing Sands, has natural arches, caves and waterfalls to explore, and there's a good three-hour walk taking in Sgorr an Fharaidh and the clifftops behind the croft.

13 Cleadale, Isle of Eigg PH42 4RL ● 01687 482480
sueeigg@gmail.com ● eiggorganics.co.uk

Open March–October.
OS Explorer map 397 (NM 478 888).
Nearest pub There's no pub on the island as such but, if you fancy a treat, the restaurant at Lageorna B&B (lageorna.com; 01687 460081) is just two minutes walk.
Access You can't take vehicles to Eigg. A minibus service travels between the pier and Cleadale twice a day. Hire bikes (eiggadventures.co.uk; 01687 347007), walk to the croft from the pier (about an hour) or stick your thumb out (residents are happy to give lifts).
Mobile phone signal You've left your car on the mainland, taken the ferry and then hiked your way across Eigg to a campsite at the foot of gigantic pitchstone cliffs. Think about it. If you're expecting even one bar of phone signal you're expecting too much.
If it's full It won't be and you'd better hope it's not. There is no other formal camping on the island. So it's wild camping or back to the ferry.

45

Long Beach Campsite

With no roads in or out, an 18-mile hike over mountains or a seven-mile sea crossing, Long Beach can claim to be the remotest campsite in Britain. The Knoydart Peninsula is known as Scotland's last great wilderness, a brooding landscape of four Munros and dramatic glens, and beaches cut off from the rest of the world. Some 17,200 acres of it is owned by a charitable trust, including Long Beach Campsite on the shores of Loch Nevis.

Rangers run this simple but effective campsite and, if you haven't pre-booked online, you can pay in the shop by the ferry quay in Inverie, just a 15-minute walk away. There's a composting loo, a UV-filtered drinking water tap and a log cabin shelter for when the wind whips up and funnels down the glen between Ladhar Bheinn and Meall Buidhe, which rise formidably behind the campsite. On calmer days, the protective crescent of the bay makes it a wonderful place to swim, looking across at the Isle of Rum on the horizon.

As well as running the campsite, the ranger service is the source of all wisdom. They look after the bird hides, offer mountain bike hire, run foraging workshops and sell maps of the various walking routes in the village shop. And, if the mountains are too imposing to tackle on your own, they also offer guided hikes. Exploring the peninsula is not for the faint of heart, however – there's no busy road or bus service to hitch a lift home on – but for the wild at heart, Knoydart is pretty perfect.

Inverie, Knoydart, Mallaig, Highlands PH41 4PL ● 01687 462242
info@knoydart.org ● knoydart.org

Open All year.
OS Explorer map 413 (NM 774 991).
Nearest pub It's a 15-minute walk back to the Old Forge (theoldforge.co.uk; 01687 462267) overlooking the quay and laying claim to the title of 'remotest pub in Britain'.
Access There are several walking routes into Knoydart, with the most popular starting at Kinlochhourn (two days, break your journey at the campsite in Barisdale) or Glenfinnan (three days, stopping at bothies or wild camping). If you are interested in walking, contact the Knoydart Foundation in advance; the rangers are able to provide help and route advice on what can be an arduous trek. Alternatively, drive to Mallaig and hop on the ferry to Inverie. From the pier, it's a 20-minute walk to the camping pitches.
Mobile phone signal Mobiles are as good as a chocolate tea pot round these parts.
If it's full Given the remote location, there's no real danger of this.

With no roads in or out, an 18-mile hike over mountains or a seven-mile sea crossing, Long Beach can claim to be the remotest campsite in Britain.

46

Dall Cottage

A certain sense of adventure comes with taking off your shoes and socks, rolling up your trousers and wading through the River Garry to your camping pitch on the other side. The water, percolating from the adjacent Munros, including A' Bhuidheanach Bheag to the west and Beinn Dear to the east, is chilly enough to send shivers up the spine. So, too, is the dramatic setting and the fact that, even on the busiest weekends, only a handful of campers get to stay here.

There are just four pitches at Dall Cottage and the only other way they can be reached is by fording the river in a four-by-four or hitching a lift with someone who has one (including helpful owner Tabitha). The result is a suitably wild and secluded space with the soporific sounds of the river to lull you to sleep and a sunrise that kisses the mountain tops to wake you. Access to a hot shower and composting toilets are the only things that add a touch of modernity to proceedings – that and the nearby A9, which lies on the civilised side of the river, ready to whisk you away to local attractions.

The Garry largely marks out the south-eastern boundary of the Cairngorms but, despite the national park's proximity, it's not the only great space to explore. Tay Forest Park and Loch Tummel are also moments away, and there's a good hike up the hill behind the campsite and over to lesser-known Loch Errochty on the other side.

Dall Cottage, Calvine, Pitlochry, Perthshire, Highlands PH18 5UL ● 07833 052506
tattyplum@yahoo.co.uk ● dallcottagecamping.business.site

Open Easter–October.

OS Explorer map OL49 (NN 758 691).

Nearest pub It's four miles to the Struan Inn (thestruan-inn.co.uk; 01796 483714), with more options if you travel another four to Blair Atholl, including a hip taproom at Wasted Degrees Brewing (wasteddegrees.com) and a quaint tearooms in the old watermill (blairathollwatermill.com; 01796 481321).

Access If you have a four-by-four with good ground clearance you can cross the river, otherwise you'll have to wade (there's a space for car parking) or get a lift with Tabitha.

Mobile phone signal There's occasional talk of people getting phone signal here but we're pretty sure it's nothing more than a mountain myth.

If it's full There's a caravan park in Blair (blaircastlecaravanpark.co.uk; 01796 481263; nine miles) but Ardgualich Farm (01796 472825; 18 miles) overlooking Loch Tummel is worth the longer drive.

*The water, percolating from the adjacent
Munros, including A' Bhuidheanach Bheag
to the west and Beinn Dear to the east, is
chilly enough to send shivers up the spine.*

47

Ace Hideaways

In the lesser-known hinterland between the Cairngorms and the coast, Ace Hideaways is an adventure-centre-cum-campsite where you can choose the wild camping experience you like. Adrenaline seekers come here for the white-water rafting, gorge walking and cliff jumping along the nearby River Findhorn, but the off-grid woodland campsite – home to just five or so pitches – is quiet enough to seek the opposite too: a sense of utter calm.

The fragrant mix of pine, larch and birch isn't overly dense, so there's plenty of light among the trees and fantastic stargazing at night. Quiet campers can watch for red squirrels or spot deer roaming across the adjacent meadow and the camping pitches – Wagtail, Buzzard, Sandpiper – are all named after birds commonly sighted here.

Facilities-wise, things are eclectic. Aside from camping pitches there are bell tents you can hire and two furnished shepherd's huts, plus compost loos and gas-heated showers. A communal area for cooking, with utensils and washing-up sinks, houses a huge log table crafted out of a giant tree that blew down on the banks of the Findhorn.

Get your bearings at Logie Steading Visitor Centre and cafe (logie.co.uk; 01309 611378), two miles away, and make your plan for the day, heading out to the coast or strolling along Sluie Walk, which leads through Darnaway forest and offers glimpses over a turbulent stretch of gorge.

Auchnagairn, Dunphail, Forres, Moray, Highlands IV36 2QL • 01309 611729
bookings@aceadventures.co.uk • acehideaways.co.uk

Open April–October.
OS Explorer map OL61 (NH 987 478).
Nearest pub The nearest pub is probably a 20–25-minute drive to Findhorn – try The Kimberley Inn (kimberleyinn.com; 01309 690492) – but there's also a good café, The Olive Tree (the-olive-tree-cafe.co.uk; 01309 611733), in Logie Steading, two miles away, and a range of artisanal shops and delis.
Access Parking by the activity centre, then a 75–250-yard walk to your pitch.
Mobile phone signal Surprisingly decent signal. You might even get 4G.
If it's full The Loft (theloft.co.uk; 01343 850111), just east of Forres, is known for its glamping accommodation, including heated and fully furnished pods, but there's also a good off-grid campsite in an adjacent meadow and light wooded area with 15 or so pitches for tents.

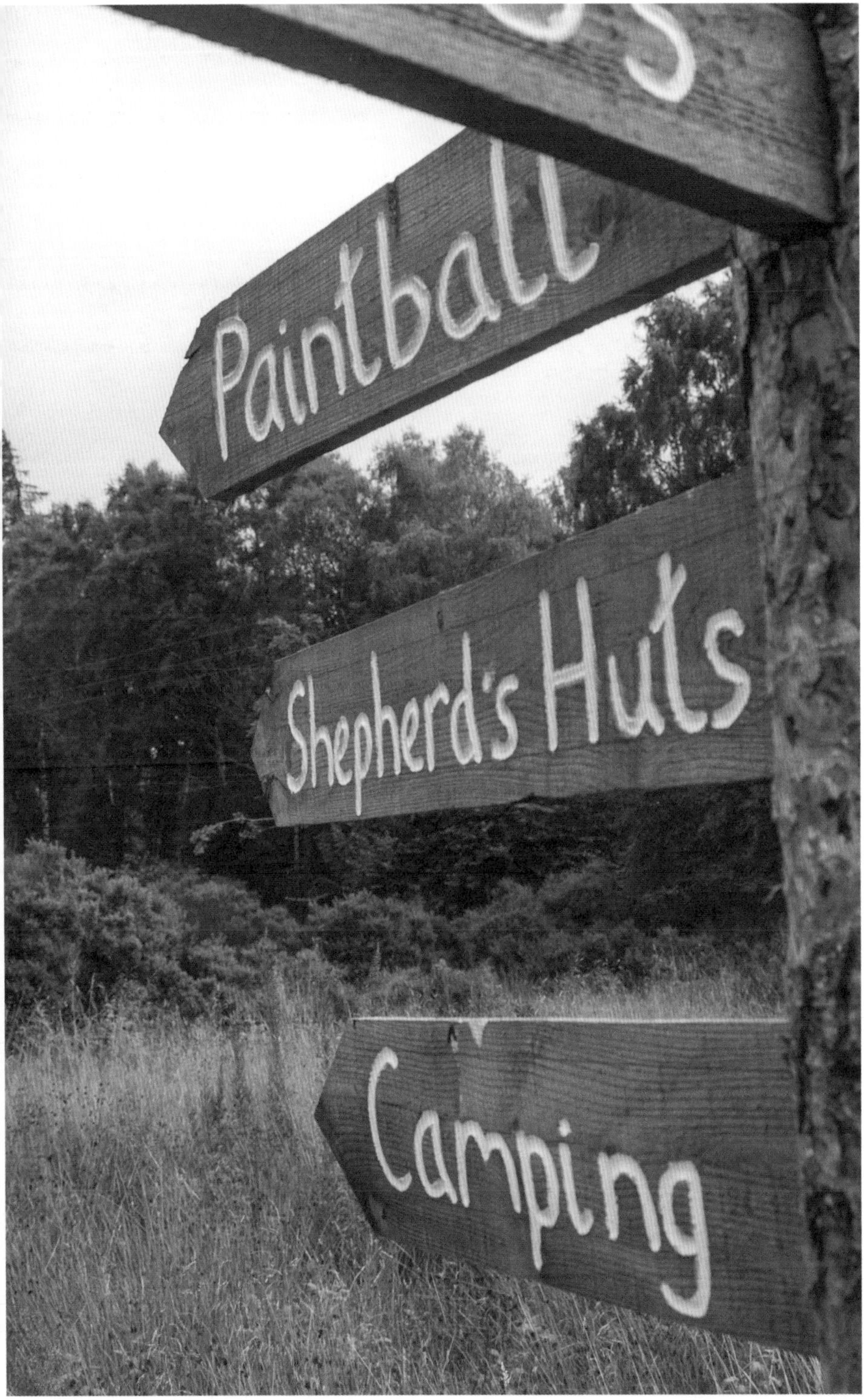
Paintball
Shepherd's Huts
Camping

48

Torridon Campsite

Despite being located just off the A896 at the entrance to Torridon village, this small field still manages to feel both incredibly remote and rustic. Rowan trees and Scots pines shield the campsite from the road, and the only facilities – a simple toilet and shower block – are actually located just outside the main gate and are also open to the general public. In keeping with the wild camping ethos, you cannot book a pitch in advance and there is no charge to stay.

The campsite's crowning glory is the voluminous Liathach massif that looms large from above the northern perimeter, although Torridon's volatile weather and frequent low cloud cover mean that you might only see the boulder fields on the mountain's lower slopes. In such overcast conditions with little wind, the midges can be ferocious, too, so be sure to bring repellent.

Torridon, a mesmerising, protected landscape of sweeping sea lochs, tumbling burns and hulking mountain peaks that vault towards the heavens, is a Mecca for walkers and climbers. Together, the Achnashellach and Torridon hills boast no less than 17 Munros. It is advisable to tackle more difficult routes in the company of a guide. Low- and high-level walks can be booked with rangers from the Countryside Centre (08444 932229) over the road from the campsite or with guides from Torridon Outdoors (thetorridon.com; 01445 791242), who also offer other activities, including sea-kayaking, gorge scrambling and guided mountain biking along the coastal trail.

Torridon, Achnasheen, Ross-shire, Highlands IV22 2EZ ● 01445 712345

Open All year.
OS Explorer map 433 (NG 905 557).
Nearest pub The Torridon Inn (thetorridon.com; 01445 791242) lies three miles from the campsite in a former stable block and has a welcoming bar and restaurant with upmarket pub grub, a good selection of real ales and over 365 whiskies to choose from.
Access It's possible to park beside your pitch but, when the ground's wet, it's better for everyone if you park at the Countryside Centre over the road (about 20 yards away).
Mobile phone signal Leading astronomers have come out unanimously to designate the campsite as a super massive black hole.
If it's full The campsite doesn't really get full, just busier and busier. If it's rammed, try one of the more formal seaside camping spots at Shieldaig Camping (shieldaigcampingandcabins.co.uk; 01520 755224), seven miles east.

49

Badrallach

Eight miles from the nearest main road and a hilly 14-mile hike to the 'local' shop, Badrallach, on the Scoraig Peninsula, is a place for campers seeking solitude or bandits on the run. If the tiny camping meadow isn't quiet enough, you can tuck yourself away at the bottom of the field among the gorse and start rustling up a campfire to keep the midges at bay – you can journey as far as you want into nowhere but they will still always manage to find you.

The most commanding feature at Badrallach is the view. The campsite occupies a rare flat space between 2,000-foot Beinn Ghobhlach and the sparkling waters of Little Loch Broom while, on the opposite shore, the sandstone hulk of An Teallach looms, a massif with no fewer than 10 distinct summits over 3,000 feet.

Those with all the gear arrive with fishing tackle or sea kayaks on their roofs and immediately make the most of the loch. A short footpath leads from the campsite down to the water's edge, while another leads five miles along the shore to the remote settlement of Scoraig. When the loch is too rough for boats, the path is Scoraig's only link with the outside world and, chances are, if the wind's that bad, it's not exactly the safest of walks either. It's swings and roundabouts with the changeable Scottish weather, however. It does wonders for Scoraig's wind turbines, which provide the majority of the community's power. And it makes the moody views from the campsite all the more wild and dramatic. With any luck it might just keep the midges at bay too.

Croft 9, Badrallach, Dundonnell, Ross-shire, Highlands IV23 2QP ● 07435 123190
mail@badrallach.com ● badrallach.com

Open All year.
OS Explorer map 435 (NH 066 917).
Nearest pub You're really in the middle of nowhere here. The Dundonnell Hotel (dundonnellhotel.com; 01854 633204) is the nearest place to get a drink, but it's more than seven miles away.
Access You can park beside your pitch in the main meadow or walk the 50–150 yards to the lower gorse pitches.
Mobile phone signal You'd be better off using a carrier pigeon.
If it's full On the opposite shore of Little Loch Broom, Northern Lights Camping (01697 371379) offers a decent, almost-wild alternative, with 15 or so pitches and relatively basic facilities; and it's well placed for climbing An Teallach.

50

Lickisto Blackhouse

Perched snugly above a sea loch at the end of what is known as 'the golden road' (not because of the views but because it cost a fortune to build across the rugged terrain), this quirky, homespun campsite has made a name for itself as the place to camp on Harris' eastern coast.

The site is not as wild as it first appears. Camping pitches are personally mown out by the owner and there are a couple of yurts for lazy bones, but pitches are all separated from each other by wild grasses, high heather, gap-toothed drystone walls and the general scoops and lumps of the landscape, giving everyone their own individual space.

Not only is Lickisto wonderfully small (around 15 pitches all told) but it also aims to be extremely low impact. The site has its own restored 200-year-old blackhouse, thatched with local heather, where you can cook a meal, have a shower or simply relax, and the wooden bridges and walkways that dot the area are made from telegraph poles discarded at the roadside by a telecoms company. You can pick veg from the site's polytunnel and catch fish down on the water's edge, where campfires are also allowed.

Come outside of summer and you're likely to be entirely alone, save for the resident ducks and, if you're lucky, the otter, who makes her evening commute back down the loch with supper in her mouth. That's what counts as rush hour at Lickisto.

1 Lickisto, Isle of Harris HS3 3EL ● 07968 951314
lickistoblackhousecamping.co.uk

Open March–October (and sometimes possible throughout the year by arrangement). **OS Explorer map** 455 (NG 119 924).
Nearest pub You're not flushed with options. Back in Tarbert there's the bar at the Harris Hotel (harrishotel.com; 01859 502154) but the best option for a pint is the hip tap room at the Loomshed Hebridean Brewery (loomshed.scot).
Access Parking (and campervan spaces) are by the road, then it's 100 yards to your pitch.
Mobile phone signal The Hebrides aren't known for their mobile coverage. The locals recommend EE or O2. We recommend a paper cup and a piece of string, which might as well be what you're using at Lickisto.
If it's full There's a fabulous and super-cheap almost-wild campsite at Ardroil Beach on Harris' west coast, cared for by the community (01851 672248). It can get busy with campervans and motorhomes in summer and end up feeling a little like a car park but there are great spots in the dunes for tents.

Almost Wild **GLAMPING**

Hot tubs? En-suite bathrooms? That doesn't sound too wild does it? Glamping has come of age in the last decade and what was, at first, just a few campsites offering pre-pitched tipis in the trees has fast become a whole new accommodation industry with even top hotels getting in on the act. As much as it pains us to admit it, though, at the end of night after night after night of nature-immersed wild camping, we don't always say no if we're offered an evening beside a log-burner and a proper bed for the night. But why not keep it wild? Even when it comes to glamping there are many sites that offer something extra to keep you truly close to nature. Perhaps it's hanging out in the trees or being totally alone in a river valley – whatever getting into the wild means to you, there might be somewhere almost wild to stay in it.

51 Cornish Yurt Holidays

Bodmin, Cornwall • 01208 850670
yurtworks.co.uk

Wake up to birdsong and go to sleep when the
last candle flickers out. The three yurts at this
site on the edge of Bodmin Moor are entirely
off grid so you soon settle into nature's rhythm.
There are bluebells in spring, butterflies in
summer and badgers make their setts down by
the River Camel, which tumbles through the site.
Each yurt is set in a private glade amid a sloping
37-acre smallholding that's part woodland, part
pasture and all about sustainability. But while it's
low on environmental impact, the yurts manage
to be rather high on comfort; each is well
furnished and warmed with a log burner and has
its own campfire area and compost loo outside.

52 Wild Boar Wood

Haywards Heath, West Sussex • 01273 980218
pegsandpitches.co.uk

It's very much back-to-basics at Wild Boar
Wood, which is run by the same people who
manage the off-grid Beech Estate campsite
in East Sussex (see p.48). Cooking is done on
campfires, showers are under buckets and you
have to wheelbarrow your kit from car to pitch.
But the nine bell tents are still pitched for you
and equipped with all the kit you'll need (except
for bedding) and loos are even of the flushing
kind. The nostalgic appeal is enhanced by old-
fashioned fun, including tree-climbing, den-
building and waving at steam trains passing on
the Bluebell Railway, which stretches along the
western perimeter of the site.

53 Lockhurst Hatch Farm

Guildford, Surrey • 01483 202689

lockhurst-hatch-farm.co.uk

A lone shepherd's hut in the corner of a field with uninterrupted views of the Surrey Hills makes up Lockhurst Hatch Farm Glamping. It may be just 30 minutes' drive from the M25 but, from here, there's not a building in sight. The hut itself has dinky proportions, perfect for a couple, with a double bed, chairs, a table and a log-burning stove. The loo outside is composting and the shower is open-air, but hot. The only other modern conveniences are a couple of guilty pleasures: the means to charge your mobile phone and a homecooked farmhouse breakfast delivered to your doorstep, substantial enough to fill you for a day in the great outdoors.

54 Gemini Camp

Stansted, Essex • 07900 200345

Fancy a safari but not the long flight? Then head to Stansted – not the airport but nearby Gemini Camp where a single bell tent sits among the long swaying grasses of a rewilded meadow. Birds and butterflies flit about while muntjac and roe deer graze under the watchful eye of whoever is lucky enough to be the sole occupant of this private six-acre nature reserve. It's a slice of wilderness not far off the beaten track; just 30 minutes from Cambridge and an hour from London. While there is the unavoidable sound from aircraft it can't take away from the other flying things you'll hear: owls, buzzards and woodpeckers among them.

55 Little Seed Field

Ripon, North Yorkshire • 07817 904339
yorkshiredalesglamping.co.uk

Five octagonal wooden cabins are bedded into
the long grasses of Little Seed Field, offering a
Hobbit-esque hideaway with views across the
Nidderdale Valley. Each is well equipped with
proper beds and a wood-burner; two even have
en-suite facilities, but, while inside there are
plenty of comforts, outside there's an intentional
commitment to keeping the surroundings wild.
The cabins are sited among boulders, trees and
rushes, which form a natural part of a Yorkshire
landscape the dairy-farm owners have tried hard
to preserve. Visiting wildlife, including deer and
birds of prey, is testament to the fact that their
work is paying off.

56 Wanderlusts Gypsy Caravans

Eden Valley, Cumbria • 07815 439130
wanderlusts.co.uk

Why settle for one glamping location when you
can roam between a few? You don't just sleep in
one of Wanderlust's handmade bow-top wagons,
you can also travel from one rustic camp to
another, helped on your way by owner Barney
and his two shire horses. This capable team have
been wandering the quiet lanes of Cumbria, and
far beyond, for 20 years and have a network of
private meadows for you to stop at. On arrival
at each pitch, Barney will help settle you in and
get your campfire started before leaving you to
enjoy the romance of the road for a night or two.

57 Red Kite Tree Tents

Powys, Mid Wales • 02921 175003
chillderness.co.uk

Follow rough tracks through this private
80-acre wood in the Cambrian Mountains
and eventually, above a bubbling brook, you'll
discover a pair of spherical globes, suspended in
the pine trees. Crafted from highbred aluminium,
canvas and steam-bent ash, these novel bedrooms
are accessed via raised platforms that include
an outdoor cooking space, a tree shower and a
long web of netting that's akin to an oversized
hammock. Off grid and off ground, the tree tents
offer a unique perspective on the local wildlife
(be sure to store your food properly when you're
done cooking) and, with phone signal crowded
out by the surrounding hills, it's an ideal place
for a thorough digital detox.

58 Trellyn Woodland

Abercastle, Pembrokeshire • 01348 837762
trellyn.co.uk

If you can't decide between beachside or
woodland wild glamping: don't. You can have
the best of both worlds at Trellyn Woodland in
Pembrokeshire, a camping and glamping site in
a sheltered woodland valley leading to the little
beach at Abercastle. The site is 16 acres and yet
there are just three yurts, two geodesic domes
and six camping pitches. In short, there's lots
of space for everyone. Each yurt and dome is
furnished and is set in its own little clearing in
the woods with a field kitchen, a campfire area
and its own toilet and shower. Firewood is free
and surfboards, wetsuits and bodyboards are all
available to borrow too.

59 Ettrick Valley Yurts

Selkirk, Scottish Borders • 01750 62331

ettrickvalleyyurts.co.uk

The authentic Mongolian yurts at Ettrick Valley seem strangely at home in this remote stretch of the Scottish Borders. The dark green exterior blends in with the surrounding scenery, while the interior, warmed by a log-burning stove, provides an ideal place to hide if the weather turns 'a bit Scottish'. Despite the well-equipped and well-furnished accommodation here, the location still gives it a wild edge. The site's three yurts are situated on the banks of Newburgh Burn, which trickles, just a few hundred yards away, into the river locally billed as 'The Wild Ettrick'. On sunny days you'll be paddling in it and on starry nights you'll be listening to it as you warm yourself by the campfire.

60 Runach Arainn

Kilmory, Isle of Arran • 01770 870515

runacharainn.com

Scythed in half by a geological fault, the 19-mile-long Isle of Arran boasts a mountainous, heather-clad north that gives way to a rolling, grassy south. Close to the southern-most tip and within walking distance of the beach, Runach Arainn is home to three yurts hidden in a small orchard. Inside, there are double beds, cooking equipment and a log-burning stove. Outside, you can hop straight on to farm tracks and footpaths, ideal for a casual stroll or light mountain biking. If you don't have your own you can hire bikes from Arran Adventure Company (arranadventure.com; 01770 302244) who can help with a whole range of outdoor pursuits.

Going wild for **CAMPERVANS**

A campervan offers the freedom of the open road with more comfort and convenience than lugging around your tent. You may not be able to access some of the more remote places that traditional camping allows but you won't have to carry all your kit, since your home is on wheels. Go wild in a campervan and you can explore more widely by travelling further – and, perhaps, with a little more style.

Is wild campervanning legal?

The rules around wild campervanning are, perhaps, even more confusing than those around wild camping. While the Scottish Land Reform Act (2003) legalised access rights to the outdoors in Scotland, including camping, it specifically excluded the right to camp in a motorised vehicle. So in Scotland, like everywhere else, you can't just park up in the wilderness where you please.

Having said that, it's not really very common to be looking to off-road in a campervan and, when it comes to going wild, it's more likely you'll be hoping to park up somewhere scenic at the side of the road, not out on a heathery hillside. There's no specific UK-wide law prohibiting parking up and sleeping in a vehicle on a public highway. The roads are subject to rules imposed by local authorities and, as long as you abide by general parking rules, parking your van should be no different to parking your car. Some areas, however, usually car parks, national parks and beauty spots, will be subject to Traffic Regulation Orders that may include a ban on overnight parking or cooking. Check signage where you're parking up if you don't want to hear the dreaded knock on the window asking you to move on in the middle of the night or, worse still, wake to a fine flapping under your windscreen wipers.

The wild campervanning code

Wherever you park up for the night, you should follow much of the same wild camping guidelines that apply to tent-based camping (see p.6). It's far more difficult to be inconspicuous in a campervan than a tent, even more so in a shiny white motorhome. So forget trying to cover your vehicle with a camo net and branches and simply park considerately. Avoid parking up to sleep in a residential area and be aware of local people and other road users. Never block a public highway and never park in passing places at the side of a road. This can lead to traffic jams and, at worse, access problems for emergency vehicles. It's also unlikely to make for a quiet night's sleep.

As with all types of wild camping, you have no specific right to camp, so if you are asked to move on, do so without argument. Better still, avoid the situation in the first place by choosing the most secluded places to park up for the night or, in popular areas, stick to using campsites.

Most campervanners find a good road trip is one where you combine nights in the wild with a night on a campsite now and then to take advantage of the facilities. Awnings, tables and chairs, washing lines and other campervanning paraphernalia aren't suitable for the side of the road and you should also save emptying grey water and chemical toilets for visits to campsites too. In some places where wild campervanning is popular, campsites will let you use their chemical disposal point and water-filling points for a small charge without having to pay a full pitch fee

FIVE TIPS FOR WILD CAMPERVANNING

▲ **Go your own way**

Unless you are heading to a specifically allocated area for overnight parking, try to choose somewhere away from other campervans and motorhomes.

▲ **Never park in a passing place**

A passing place is part of the highway that has been built to help traffic flow. Parking in one of these on a single-track road is like parking in the middle of the road – and it's illegal.

▲ **Ask at the local pub**

Pub landlords will often let you stay in their car park if you pay for a meal in the pub and act responsibly while on site. If not, they are often great sources of information and might point you in the right direction.

▲ **Mix campsites with your wild camping**

Plan a stay or a visit to a campsite every few days to help support the local economy and for refilling water and emptying chemical toilets and grey water.

▲ **Leave no trace**

Leave the place you stay at exactly as you found it. Campa.org.uk offers guidance for campervanners in Scotland but its common sense advice is useful for driving anywhere.

Where to go wild campervanning

There's a reason why the classic Volkswagen campervan is so associated with surfers. It's the perfect way to stay, with all your kit, as close to the surf as possible, which means you can get in the water at sunrise or stay in until it sets. The same goes for any outdoor adventure; whether you're hiking, climbing, cycling or canoeing, the van offers the space to store your gear, a place to lay your head and a way to stay near the starting point. But sometimes the van itself provides the adventure and there are some gloriously scenic driving routes which make for great road trips. As ever, the most scenic part of the UK, national parks and Areas of Outstanding Natural Beauty, are generally the places subject to the strictest regulations and may not be the easiest places to park up in overnight.

In areas where roadside overnight parking or wild campervanning has become particularly popular and, sadly, sometimes problematic, locals and authorities have started using the terms 'layby camping' and 'fly camping', which gives you an idea of the tension between groups. There are some places where designated overnight parking is allowed; take advantage of these if you want to visit these areas and pay any associated charges to help with the upkeep and protection for future use. We'll not be recommending specific places to park up here (there are plenty of good online resources for this, including campa.org.uk, thecampervana.com and the park4night app), instead we encourage you to use this book as a how-to rather than a where-to guide; turn off the SatNav and go where the road takes you. Just like with wild camping, the quietest spots are often the ones you find yourself.

Going wild for **CAMPFIRES**

Camping without a campfire is like tea without sugar – thoroughly enjoyable but not quite as sweet. At the most basic level, a campfire is a source of heat, light and a means of cooking your dinner but for many of us, it's much more than that. Crackling flames, the smell of wood smoke, a lovely warm glow and the conversations that flow around it mean your campfire is your entertainment for the night too: absorbing, enchanting and mesmerising in equal measure.

The joy of a campfire

There's no denying the joy of a campfire. As the first embers spark the first flames you can't help but feel like a bit of a hero. No matter how many times you've coaxed a fire into life, there's a kind of primeval satisfaction that doesn't diminish. Once you're satisfied it's not going to go out, you can settle back and enjoy the flames: cook on them, toast marshmallows on them and gaze into them. The heat, warmth and light lets you stay up later and experience things you might otherwise miss. Listen for owls, look for shooting stars and generally feel closer to nature. If you're alone, the fire is a comfort and if you're with friends it's a focus. Ideas, conversation and stories are more easily shared around a campfire and silences never seem awkward. Sound too magical to be true? There's only one way to find out...

Wild camping and campfires

Before you move on to starting your campfire, know that with great joy comes great responsibility. Fires are inevitably high risk and need to be managed carefully. If you're camping on a campsite, follow the site guidelines and if you're camping wild, well, ideally, don't have one. It is part of wild camping etiquette that you leave no trace. That inevitably includes no scorch marks on the ground, no destruction of habitat through the collection of deadwood and no burning of vegetation. In short: no campfires. The romantic ideal of a campfire under a starry night sky is, unfortunately, best kept for the campsite. Designated firepit areas and sustainable wood supplies help keep environmental damage to a minimum and (while we hate to bring health and safety into it) there will likely be some fire safety measures in place too. When you're wild camping, stick to the camping stove or, if it's just not camping without a campfire, head to one of the almost wild campsites in this book instead.

8 Steps to a successful campfire – burn after reading

▲ **Go prepared:** don't forget matches, a lighter or a fire striker (maybe even all three).

▲ **Use an existing firepit or prepare the ground:** dig a shallow pit away from any combustible vegetation and ring it with stones if possible.

▲ **Gather your tinder** (newspaper, birch bark or pine cones), kindling (small dry sticks) and logs.

▲ **Make an airy structure** in the middle of your firepit with pieces of kindling around a little of your tinder material; a pyramid is traditional but a lattice leaning against or on top of two logs works well too.

▲ **Lean three or four larger pieces of firewood** in a loose pyramid shape around your kindling structure.

▲ **Light the tinder** material at the centre of your structure.

▲ **Watch as the tinder burns** and lights the kindling, then the larger logs in turn.

▲ **Enjoy your campfire.**

REMEMBER: Avoid lighting fires when you're wild camping – use a camping stove for cooking and preparing hot drinks instead.

Being able to light a fire is a basic life skill, one of the things that sets us humans apart from the beasts. In theory, we should all be able to do it with ease. Unfortunately, the reality is that, unless you are a super-regular camper who has honed your firelighting skills over years, it's likely to take a few failed attempts at a campfire before you get reliable flames. Damp ground, wind, rain and, sometimes, just the added pressure of being watched can thwart attempts at getting your fire going in the great outdoors. But, just because sparks don't fly on the first attempt, it doesn't mean you should give up. Starting a campfire, however you choose to do it, takes a little bit of preparation and a calm, careful approach; not to mention a spark, some tinder, kindling, wood and airflow.

Four natural firelighters

Forget chemical firelighters and use one of nature's firelighters instead – eco friendly, often readily available and completely free!

Birch bark

Pine cones

King Alfred's Cake (a small black fungus that grows on dead wood)

Horse hoof fungus (a large semi-circular, brown woody fungus which grows on trees)

Remember, the cumulative effect of foraging can be destructive. Ask the campsite owner before collecting firewood or natural firelighters and collect only what you need and will use.

Campfire cooking

What could possibly be more satisfying than getting a campfire going? The answer, of course, is cooking your dinner on it. Whether it's a can of beans cooked in their tin, a fancy three-course feast in the wild or something in between, campfire cooking is a skill worth mastering. A hot meal can make or break a camping trip, making hangry campers into happy campers who are hungry for more.

If you've ever cooked on a barbecue, there's nothing to fear from campfire cooking as the experience is not all that different. Charcoal is usually swapped for wood but the key is to wait until you have hot embers and not to attempt to get that flame-grilled flavour by sticking your sausages (or anything else) straight into a just-lit fire. You can grill, stew or even roast on a campfire if you know how but if you're dipping a toe into the world of campfire cooking for the first time it's a good idea to keep things relatively simple.

A jacket potato and baked beans is about the easiest campfire meal you can make – and, handily, one of the most satisfying too. It also ticks another box for campers who like going back to basics; it is easy to transport and requires no refrigeration. Just don't forget the tin opener or the foil. You may want to take things up a notch from a jacket spud, perhaps a one-pot stew, for example, but this teaches an important lesson: preparation is as key to campfire cooking as it is to starting the campfire. You can head off from camp to buy what you need, but you might find yourself limited to putting a sausage on a stick or buying a lot of things you'll end up throwing away. Don't leave things to chance. Plan what you're going to cook and take the pots, pans and utensils you need from home along with oil, salt, pepper, stock, spices or condiments for a more sensible and sustainable campfire dinner. Bon appétit!

Bushcraft courses in the UK

▲ **Woodland Ways – Fire Lighting Bushcraft Weekend**
A three-day course focusing on fire at Appleton in
Oxfordshire or Haddon Hall in Derbyshire.
woodland-ways.co.uk

▲ **Bushcraft Skills and Survival Weekends**
Bushcraft and survival skills courses in England
and Scotland. wildwoodbushcraft.com

▲ **Woodlore Bush Chef with Ray Mears**
A three-day campfire cookery course is one of a number of
bushcraft courses with the Woodlore legend Ray Mears in
East Sussex. www.raymears.com

Going wild for **LOCAL**

Wherever and however you travel, the joy of visiting new places is in experiencing new things and, for a true taste of a destination, there's no substitute for tapping into local knowledge. It can open up a world of experiences that you might otherwise miss and give a greater understanding of the destinations you visit. By living like a local you're also likely to have a bigger impact on the local economy and a smaller one on the environment. It's the most sustainable and enjoyable way to stay.

Ask a local

It's a rare occasion these days when you can't just ask Google for the answer but, when the question is about a hidden local treasure or even just the best place for coffee, it's better to ask a local. It's often the businesses with the biggest budget that attract attention online rather than the homespun independents that you'd really love to find. Ask around locally and you're more likely to get the information that you crave.

When you're staying on a campsite, you often have access to a ready-made local expert in the form of your campsite host. They should be able to point you in the direction of a good walk, a great pub or the best local beach. If you're camping wild, however, it can be harder to know who to ask. The local pub, shop or café might yield some results from punters as well as staff but, if the real world doesn't offer any answers, the digital one might. Rather than asking Google, try social media. Follow hashtags for the area you're visiting to find organisations and people who are regularly posting about what's going on and you'll soon find the local zeitgeist.

Local guides

A guided tour doesn't have to mean being part of a big group, following someone around a city with a yellow umbrella held aloft. There are plenty of local enthusiasts out there who will take you on a tour to show you a wilder side of local life, often in smaller groups or as part of a tailored experience. Forest schools, bushcraft experts, local wildlife trusts and nature-based organisations are all great places to look to learn about different aspects of the local environment.

If you have a specific interest in climbing, cycling, sailing or any other activity, try contacting organisations in the area you're visiting to see if any of their members are keen to share their knowledge. Even the more traditional tourism and destination management organisations, like Visit Britain and its subsidiaries, have a greater focus on experiences these days, and campsite owners are generally in the know of local mountain or kayaking guides they can put you in touch with.

Local food – straight from the source

Pasties from Cornwall, cave-aged cheese from Cheddar and oysters from Whitstable… food can tell you a lot about the places you visit. It's tied up in the local landscape, indicative of its industries and a thoroughly enjoyable way to get stuck into a place. Seek out micropubs, freehouses, independent cafés and farm shops and you'll get a better taste of the area than if you call in at a big-brand coffee shop and stock up in the supermarket. Best of all is when you can buy straight from the source; from a farm shop that's selling produce grown or reared just fields away or a fisherman selling straight from the boat. There's no denying that produce will be fresher and always tastes better when it's consumed on home turf.

You might even be able to learn about or get involved in the local food production process, with more and more local producers offering the chance to see behind the scenes. There are tours and tastings at vineyards and microbreweries, and courses in everything from cheesemaking and breadmaking to fishing and foraging. Get involved in the local food scene and you'll probably have a great day out. You'll almost definitely have a delicious dinner and you might also get a warm fuzzy feeling, safe in the knowledge that you are helping to build a more sustainable tourism economy for the place that you're visiting.

FIVE FARMS **WHERE YOU CAN BUY FROM SOURCE**

▲ Fen Farm Dairy, Suffolk

A dairy farm in Bungay, Suffolk with a cow-print shed housing what is said to be the UK's first raw milk vending machine. You can fill your own bottle (or buy one of theirs) and watch through the windows of the dairy where the Fen Farm team might be making their raw-milk cheese, butter or skyr, Icelandic yoghurt – also on sale here.
fenfarmdairy.co.uk

▲ Nightingale Cider Company, Kent

Home-grown seasonal fruit and vegetables are sold here plus, as the name suggests, cider and juice, made from apples grown in the farm's orchard. A range of goods from other local producers are also sold in this extensive farm shop that's been championing local produce for over 20 years.
nightingalecider.com

▲ The Blagdon Farm Shop, Newcastle-upon-Tyne

For fresh produce it's hard to beat The Blagdon Farm Shop, where just-picked veg can be on sale just 15 minutes after it's been picked. Meat from the Blagdon Estate is also available from the onsite butchery and there's a bakehouse selling homecooked, small batch meals and goodies too.
theblagdonfarmshop.co.uk

▲ High Weald Dairy, Sussex

A wide range of award-winning cheeses, many organic, are produced at the High Weald Dairy in Sussex, based on a family-owned dairy farm. There's no formal shop but you're welcome to pop in and buy from the farm office. Book in advance for a tour of the dairy to see the cheese-making in action.
highwealddairy.co.uk

▲ The Beacons Farm Shop, Powys

On the edge of the Brecon Beacons National Park, The Beacons Farm Shop specialises in selling venison and other meats. You can see deer and sheep grazing in the fields around the shop which also sells other local produce and, to top it off, there's a café on site.
beaconsfarmshop.co.uk

Going wild for **SWIMMING**

There's a wild swimming revolution going on in the UK, with more and more people choosing to make a splash in natural surroundings. Whether it's plunging into an icy mountain tarn, doing a lap of a lake, swimming gently along a river or just taking a dip in the sea, there's something invigorating, purifying and addictive about swimming wild.

> *"I wanted to follow the rain on its meanderings about our land to rejoin the sea, to break out of the frustration of a lifetime doing lengths, endlessly turning back on myself like a tiger pacing its cage."*

Roger Deakin, *Waterlog: A Swimmer's Journey Through Britain*

The rise and rise of wild swimming

"I wanted to follow the rain on its meanderings about our land to rejoin the sea, to break out of the frustration of a lifetime doing lengths, endlessly turning back on myself like a tiger pacing its cage." So said wild swimming pioneer Roger Deakin in his book *Waterlog: A Swimmer's Journey Through Britain*. His words elegantly capture the freedom that wild swimming offers to its ever-increasing number of converts. Numbers have been on the rise for a couple of decades but reached a peak in 2020 when Covid-19 meant that indoor pools had to close. More and more swimmers, desperate to get in the water, took to wild swimming in the warmer months and, for many of them, once acclimatised, there was no turning back.

Part of the joy of wild swimming is that it's unsupervised and unsanitised but, of course, that brings with it an element of risk. Before taking the plunge into the nearest lake or stream it's worth reading up and making sure that you are aware of the potential dangers of wild swimming generally and your chosen location specifically. As long as you are a competent swimmer and take good care in choosing when and where you swim, there's little to fear and lots to look forward to.

Swimming safely

There's no chlorine to chemically clean the water in the great outdoors so it's well worth checking the water quality both by eye, on signs in location and online (see resources on p.184). Generally avoid canals, stagnant water, urban areas and swimming after heavy rain. Heavy rainfall can cause pollutants to wash into the waterways but it also adds another danger of fast-flowing water. Wherever you swim, check the water flow before you get in. Avoid places with fast flow and strong currents and be wary that not all currents are visible from the surface. Swimming above a big waterfall is not a very sensible idea.

You should check the temperature and the depth of water before diving or jumping in. In fact, there may not be a lifeguard to blow the whistle at you but jumping and diving are generally frowned upon. After just a few wild swims you start to acclimatise to cold water and can enjoy the invigoration it brings but, at first, you should make sure to enter the water slowly. You should also get out if you don't warm up after a few minutes or once you start getting cold again. Dry off, put warm clothes on quickly and perhaps move about to help blood flow. A warm drink helps too, helping heat you up from the inside. The best piece of safety advice, however, is not to swim alone; take a friend along to swim with you or even just to hold your towel. You'll lifeguard each other and, you never know, you might find yourself having twice the fun.

RESOURCES FOR MORE INFORMATION ON WILD SWIMMING

▲ *Waterlog* by Roger Deakin

Generally considered the wild swimmer's bible, this renowned piece of nature writing by the late wild swimmer and environmentalist Roger Deakin charts his 1996 journey swimming through Britain.

▲ **The Outdoor Swimming Society**

A volunteer-led society that's free to join, celebrating outdoor swimming. The OSS, founded by Kate Rew, author of the book *Wild Swim*, also organises open-water swimming events.
outdoorswimmingsociety.com

▲ **Wild Swim**

A crowd-sourced swim map (temporarily suspended during the coronavirus pandemic due to demand) showcasing UK wild swim locations with contributions from the wild swimming community.
wildswim.com

▲ **Wild Swimming**

A community-fed website with information on open-water swimming and a swim map, started by Wild Things Publishing.
wildswimming.co.uk

▲ **Swim the Lakes**

A private company offering guided open-water swims in the Lake District, plus free online advice on swimming in the national park.
swimthelakes.co.uk

▲ **Surfers Against Sewage**

An environmental charity that keeps a close eye on pollutants in our coastal waters. Get its award-winning app, Safer Seas Service, for real-time information on water quality.
sas.org.uk

▲ **Royal Life Saving Society**

Safety tips for all types of swimming from a charity that provides training in water safety. Their website has a useful and specific section on safety in open-water swimming.
rlss.org.uk

What to look for in a wild swimming spot

With safety considerations in mind, choosing a wild swimming spot becomes a matter for personal taste. Outside of urban areas and private property, the waterways are yours to explore. Do you prefer mountain scenery or gently rolling hills? Farmland, fenland, woods or moors? An open lake or a winding river? There's water, water everywhere – once you start to look, so you can start your search with a view to the scenery you'd like to see. On arrival, make sure you've investigated the safety side of things so you know where you can get in and out of the water safely and that the water does not pose a danger in any of the ways listed on p.183.

If you're just starting out, you might like to begin at the tame end with a dip in a warm shallow lake, a lifeguarded beach or, perhaps, even a lido during summer. There are also plenty of groups of outdoor swimmers who take to the water en masse and you might feel more confident by joining one to start with. Organised events for open-water swimmers are another way to meet like-minded waterbabies. If you prefer to swim alone or with just a friend or two, you can still make use of the wild swimming community's combined knowledge by searching online swim maps and lists of recommendations for popular and not-so-popular swimming spots (see resources opposite).

Going wild for **THE PLANET**

We are at a pivotal moment in history, with the human impact on the planet more evident than ever before. It's long been a mantra of wild campers and nature lovers to 'leave no trace' but, if we want to continue enjoying our natural surroundings, we should be thinking about doing more. We need to take positive action: to enhance, not just conserve, and to mitigate the damage already done. There's never been a more important time to protect the wild and we all have a part to play.

Consider your impact on people and places

Our holidays cost more than just the money we pay for them. They have an environmental cost too, and if you're looking to have a truly sustainable camping trip you should think about paying for that – and, perhaps, adding a tip. There's a carbon footprint to mitigate, which comes not only from the way we travel to our holiday location but also from the things we buy and consume while we're there. Then there's a physical footprint and even a legacy that we leave behind through our behaviour.

Camping is one of the most eco-friendly ways to holiday, so the environmental cost, like the monetary one, is relatively low. For those who love camping, it sounds like a win–win situation but low impact does not mean no impact and there are still costs to consider. The least we can do is to leave a pitch (wild or otherwise) as we found it, leaving no trace that we were ever there. The starting point is relatively simple: take away all your belongings and rubbish, including any tiny bits of plastic or foil. You should make sure any fire is fully extinguished and that the remains of any firepit are cleared or covered. But going a little further is not hard to do and it's often enjoyable too. How about extending your litter pick beyond the bounds of your camp, using observations from your trip to contribute to a conservation project or planting a tree somewhere to replace any firewood used? (See p.189 for a few ideas.)

Sustainable travel to protect the wild

Travelling to your campsite can be one of the biggest environmental costs but there are lots of ways to reduce it. How about camping closer to home? The most sustainable way to travel is to go back to basics and walk. Travel on your own two feet and you will leave only footprints – but you won't be able to get very far either. For some lucky people, walking from home to your pitch for the night is perfectly possible but if you live in a city that's unlikely to be the case. There's always cycling and, for the super-fit and super-light traveller, a bike can be a fantastic way to travel to your destination and to get around when you arrive. It's less accessible and more limiting with kids but far from impossible, especially with careful planning.

Where walking and cycling are not practical, the next most sustainable way to travel to a campsite is by public transport. Take the train or bus rather than your own car and the carbon footprint is reduced. It also combines well with walking and cycling trips that you might want to make in destinations further from home. For families and for longer trips to places that are off the beaten track, driving can seem like the only workable solution but you can still work at using the car less for shorter journeys once there. As we get closer to 2030, when the UK government has promised to end the sale of new petrol and diesel cars, it is likely that more and more of us will be using electric and hybrid vehicles, which will make driving less polluting. If you don't own your own car, there are now plenty of e-cars and even a smattering of all-electric campervans available to hire – many of the latter can be found on our website, coolcamping.com.

Shop sustainably

Whether you're wild camping locally or flying off to Spain, it's easy to get carried away buying new things. You might not need flip flops for wild camping but you could fancy a new bivvy bag or ground mat. No matter where you're going, think before you buy. Try to shop sustainably wherever possible or perhaps don't shop at all. Reusing, repurposing, borrowing and buying secondhand are all better for the environment than buying new. Even mainstay camping brands like Vango now sell reused and second-hand equipment (see campingrecycled.co.uk). If you do need to buy new, try to choose a company with good green credentials; somewhere that offsets its carbon footprint, uses recycled materials and takes its responsibility to the planet and people seriously.

The same rules can be applied once you are on your holiday and, thankfully, buying from independent shops is a great way to shop sustainably. Choose to buy your sausages from a local farm shop instead of a supermarket and you will be supporting a local producer, reducing carbon emissions from transporting goods and, best of all, you will have fresh, regional bangers for your barbecue.

SIX WAYS TO GIVE BACK WHEN YOU'RE CAMPING WILD

▲ **Join The 2 Minute Foundation**

The 2 Minute Foundation encourages people to take part in a two-minute beach clean or litter pick wherever they are to stop pollutants entering the sea and damaging the marine environment. It's a manageable, tangible way to help clean up the environment. Join the foundation to learn more and log your cleans. **beachclean.net**

▲ **Go the Slow Way**

Use Slow Ways to get to your camping pitch and use your camping trip to contribute to the Slow Ways network. It's a map of walking routes connecting villages, towns and cities in the UK, helping people to get between destinations the slow way. Routes need to be checked, verified and monitored by volunteers. **slowways.uk**

▲ **Get the eBird app**

Log the birds you spot on your wild camping trip via the eBird app and you will be contributing to an open data source that is available to scientists and conservationists. The app lets you keep a log of all the birds you see while feeding into a worldwide project led by the Cornell Lab of Ornithology. **ebird.org**

▲ **Measure light pollution**

Globe at Night is another citizen-science project that encourages individuals to contribute data to a conservation project. This one is aimed at reducing light pollution by raising awareness of the impact it has. To take part, you merely need to stargaze and record the constellations you see from the location you are in. **globeatnight.org**

▲ **Plant a tree**

In the spirit of leaving no trace, planting a tree may not be the right thing to do in the place that you camp, but how about offsetting the impact of collecting firewood by planting one elsewhere? If you can't do this yourself, you can donate to a charity or organisation that will do this on your behalf. The World Land Trust is one such charity, and you can also learn about carbon emissions from other activities on their website. **worldlandtrust.org**

▲ **WWOOFing**

The WWOOFing movement offers opportunities for people to travel, stay, work and learn about life on organic farms and smallholdings. It's an international network pairing up volunteer workers with landowners who need help and are happy to share knowledge on sustainable living. **wwoofinternational.org**

Index

Acknowledgements

Almost Wild Camping
Editor: James Warner Smith
Series Editor: Jonathan Knight
Written by: James Warner Smith, Amy Woodland
Additional contributions from: Keith Didcock, Jenny McKelvie, Robin McKelvie,
Andy Stothert
Designer: Roamland Studio
Proofreader: Leanne Bryan, Lauren Green
Index: Helen Snaith
With additional thanks to: Lauren Ash, Patrick Beddow, Jamie Cash, Lucy Clinch,
Andrew Day, Boryana Dimitrova, Martin Dunford, Kenny Grant, Catherine Greenwood,
Neil Holland, Victoria Jackson, Brogan Kirby, Katarzyna Kolny, Grace O'Mahony,
Chris Perry, Cameron Watson

Published by: Punk Publishing,
81 Rivington Street, London EC2A 3AY

UK Sales: Compass IPS Limited, Great West House, Great West Road, Brentford TW8 9DF;
020 8326 5696; sales@compass-ips.co.uk

Front cover photograph: Kintra Farm (p.136) © Andy Stothert

The publishers and authors have done their best to ensure the accuracy of all information
in *Almost Wild Camping*, however, they can accept no responsibility for any injury, loss
or inconvenience sustained by anyone as a result of information contained in this book.
We advise checking the latest laws regarding trespass and wild camping before camping
anywhere other than a licensed campsite.